TEARS
Behind t

C000079307

J o k é   H o e t m e r

One woman's extraordinary journey of self-discovery; of finding true love and purpose... Joké's decisions invited blame and shame into her life, with many twists and turns, traumas, conflicts, self-doubts and both physical and mental abuse, not to mention the kind of rejection and betrayal that so many of today's women will recognise from their own *tears behind the smile*.

Book design by: SWATT Books Ltd

Printed in the United Kingdom
First Printing, 2022

ISBN: 978-1-7392072-0-5 (Paperback)
ISBN: 978-1-7392072-1-2 (eBook)

Joké Hoetmer
Portsmouth, Hampshire

action4life@gmail.com

Disclaimer

Some names have been changed to protect the persons involved. Similarly, sequences of events are not always described according to the true timeline, as chapters are organised by subject matter rather than chronological order. All personal stories are faithful to my memories of these experiences, presented as my truth after years of being asked to put them to paper. The perspective and persuasion I had at the time of writing was, rightly or wrongly, part of my journey, written out of love, as raw and real as possible, with the sole purpose of giving value and hope to the reader.

Clarification

This book is my story, my journey, which possibly, or maybe even probably, will seem like a description of lifestyles, environments and situations that are completely alien to those from different countries and cultures. However, the abuse I suffered – physical, mental and emotional – has no cultural, status or sex relevance. What I've shared in the following pages shows that abuse exists in all cultures, languages and religions, with the message being that only by embracing the truth of what we experience can we unite in courage and move forward to find the life of fulfilment we were robbed of.

Then, **WE** can say:

> *'I now realise I am innocent, with no obligation to accept blame or shame. I am not a victim, but a victor, who is willing to step out of hiding and into my true self-respect and sense of value!'*

Dedication

This book is dedicated to my children who have encouraged me to write the stories that even they never knew, with the faith and trust of helping others finding themselves in these painful situations. My family, my friends and the mentors who have supported me over the years, as well as the many women who have suffered and are suffering today.

A special thank you to Paul Hickman, who saw the vision and the impact of my stories. It was Paul's dedication, love and support that got me through the writing of this book when I most needed it.

You may not be able to control every situation and outcome,
but you can control your attitude and how you deal with it

I am just a woman with a past, and a hope for the future...

Your life is your life, it is unique to you. Every decision you make, no matter how small, affects how you live your life today and tomorrow. Next time you look in the mirror, ask yourself these serious questions: who are you really? Who and what are most important in your life? How is your past impacting you today? Could this be the time to step out of your past and learn to live again, fully, becoming the real you?

My raw and real life's journey will hopefully become an example to all women who have suffered, and who continue to suffer, the injustices of bullying, control and abuse; who have accepted this abuse as the norm, forsaking their right to speak out about what is happening to them behind closed doors. My aim is to help them discover a new way of living by developing the inner resilience and creating their very own *Fightback Muscle*, putting the smile back in their hearts with no tears behind it. No more hurting to barely survive, but instead allowing themselves to heal their brokenness in the knowledge that they have value and are loved, and understanding how nothing that has happened to them has to define who they are.

Remembering you are seen, and heard, and most of all loved just the way you are!

I see and hear you. (Yes, you!)

Love and hugs,

Jodie Hoetmer

What people have said about Joké

Joké has the heart of an angel, and she would do anything to protect her loved ones! She has faced hurdles larger than most, but through her perseverance and strength, she has overcome them. She is like a beacon of hope to those that know her as she always smiles through the rain. Joké does have a habit of saying "yes" to a lot of responsibilities, but she always manages to get things done. Joké knows how to lead because she is familiar with the road out of the dark times. She is loyal to her friends, and would never betray their trust.

Joké has a heart like wildfire, all passion and courage and strength. She can't be stopped when she believes in something and sets her heart on it. She's faced nightmare as dark as midnight, but it was never enough to break her down. Joké is a leader, with a soul filled with compassion and kindness. She doesn't see the world the same way others do, but exactly that is her advantage.

Joké could brighten your day with her smile. She's not afraid to feel it all. She lives, she laughs, and she cries too. Joké is a dreamer who is destined to achieve her goals. Despite everything she's been through, she still has a generous heart and a kind soul. Joké is a fire that can't be tamed – beautiful to watch.

Joké has a big heart, and she always makes sure to put the people she cares about first! She is stronger that anyone knows, but although she hides it, she has a sweet and sensitive side! Sometimes, Joké divides her attention between too many things, but she always finds a way to get things done. Joké is an excellent leader because there is simply no way to fool her! She has no place in her life for drama queens and fakes. She rarely holds a grudge, but when she does, it's because you deserve it.

Contents

Who is Joké Hoetmer?

At the age of 64, Joké was the senior matron at a retirement village in South Africa, responsible for 120 self-contained flats housing semi-active couples, plus a hospital section of 90 beds, 43 of which held bedridden patients requiring specialised nursing care. Eventually, she started to question the point of her life, asking herself:

'Is this really what my life is all about – a life that has been full of adventure, trauma and pain? Working in a place where I could be one step away from becoming an inpatient?'

Doubting her very reason for existence, feeling hopelessly lost in a life not worth the past she had overcome, she struggled to make sense of it all. Then, she heard a still, small voice say: **'STEP OUT OF THE BOAT!'**

Knowing instinctively that this was the voice of God – as there was no way she could have thought, or even imagined, such a thing on her own, with this life being all she knew – she sold all of her possessions and found herself on a plane to London with nothing except a 30kg suitcase, laptop and phone, embarking upon a journey to find her life's purpose with a childlike hope, much to the amazement and distress of the children and grandchildren she left behind.

Eight years of adjusting to her new life and self-realisation later, having accepted for the first time the healing from all the trauma and loss, and allowing herself to embrace the unhealed hurts and stepping into her *Purpose Boots*, in the hope of transforming other women from despair to hope in their loss and pain, and to achieve the fullness of their own purpose.

During this time, Joké also became a seasoned and intuitive business visionary, a public speaker and a Path to Purpose mentor, using her wealth of real-life experience to support and mentor entrepreneurs and their families through navigating and overcoming adversity, trauma, loss and pain.

Having successfully founded and established numerous companies throughout her business career, and experienced first-hand the life-altering process of entrepreneurship and the resourcefulness it requires – even while her world was collapsing around her – hers is a story of courage in the face of great obstacles.

Joké's journey of self-discovery and finding the true meaning of love and life's purpose...

Using her skills and experience, she powerfully facilitated the shifting of negative programming and inner transformation for global change-makers, masterfully impacting and influencing others through community-building and accountability, providing tools and strategies to grow lives and businesses. However, the love journey has many twists and turns; tears, traumas, rejections and betrayals; and feelings of conflict, shame and constant self-doubt continued to loom in her subconscious mind.

In the end, she chose to embrace the pain, the lessons and the journey with a drive to always do the right thing, enduring dramatic experiences in a way that she hopes will inspire the reader through its endearing honesty in describing her journey to find hope, peace and the meaning of her life.

The life lessons she learned along the way are at once practical, truthful and amusing, especially as she began to understand the reality of the situation she found herself in. Never giving up on her quest to find the truth, she bounced back with a resilience and a sense of almost childlike optimism that lasted until the next lesson came along.

Her natural curiosity and sense of adventure have placed her in many precarious situations where her innate tenacity was the only hope for survival, and she is now ready to share the secrets of this success with a wisdom reserved for everyone who knows deep down that there is more to life than what they are experiencing right now.

'The quest to love, live and laugh again carries within it the truth that, no matter what, there is a pot of gold at the end of every rainbow.'

Hope always prevails...

... this is only a season, and there is a reason for the season, and lessons to learn.

On her *Raw & Real Conversations* podcast, Joké shares her personal life stories, adventures and unusual experiences with the world, inspiring and motivating others on their paths to healing and wholeness. This journey in hindsight has been remarkable for the many people that were with her or watching her at the times in question. It was they who helped her to get out the boat and start swimming again until she arrived at a point in her life where the tide began to turn, bringing her hope, love and an expectation of helping other women to ditch the 'life belt' and start moving freely through even the choppiest waters...

'... *To fight back and stand up again, and boldly step into both her "now" and her future, wiser, stronger self with hope; finding a smile on her heart, rather than behind her tears.*'

Joké comes to you with an open mind, an open heart and the commitment to support women on their unique journeys, reaffirming that they are not alone. Woman can reach out and be encouraged to hold her hand as they step out of their own boat, embracing the unhealed hurts and becoming empowered to step into their own **Purpose Boots** through identifying with Joké's trials and tribulations.

May they be healed of their mental and emotional scars, as they find the fullness of their purpose.

Scan the QR code to get in contact with Joké direct:

The only really bad mistake
is the one you don't learn from

JOKÉ HOETMER

Why have I written this book now?

W hat I have endured and overcome would be useless if the lessons were only for me to learn; if I did not share these real-life experiences to help other women who have, like me, suffered in silence.

My life experiences would be tragic if I did not share them as a message of hope. All my pain and victories would be worthless.

What a waste of a life that would be!

Although my today is certainly not defined by my past, I know that somebody, somewhere, is looking desperately for hope in the eye of their own personal storm; suffering from physical, mental or emotional bullying and abuse; loss, betrayal or a lack of support; hiding in shame and hopelessness, trapped in their pain, with no future to look forward to.

Crying their own tears behind their smiles.

Always answering 'I'm fine,' when asked how they are, when in reality they are screaming 'Help me!'

This book was written to encourage women to share their stories, so that others can identify with the many different conflicts they have endured, as we pave the way for others to make their journeys towards becoming loved and valued for who they really are, and to find the honesty that will lead them to hope and peace.

Greatness is discovering the best version of yourself. Letting nobody define or dim your light. Lighting up your heart to laugh again, just by being you.

My wish for this book is that all those abused woman and men will use it to rise above their now and step out into a new future, by choosing to embrace the pain, the lessons and the struggles of their past. My challenge to them is to always do the right thing, even if it means putting them in the firing line, as it was this fearless approach that always allowed them to be the winner in the end.

This is a story of getting up off the floor and starting all over, fighting one more round, however big or small, because life must go on. It's about refusing to tolerate defeat and developing what I call...

The Fightback Muscle

The greatest gift you can give yourself is to develop your own ability to listen to the divine intelligence within you. Listen to that still, small voice.

I learned to listen to those close to me, those I truly admired, and became encouraged and inspired by them, as I took on board their real-life experiences and adapted them to my own unique circumstances. Now, after serving my time as the student, I am ready to become the teacher by presenting those same circumstances for others to learn from, as a beacon of hope for all the many women who silently endure injustices in their lives that nobody should accept as the norm.

Truth is discovered by harnessing the survival skills forged in the many different scenarios and circumstances of abuse experienced by other women in the past, and using them to create a brighter future wearing a smile on your heart.

> *Remember:*
> *You did not wake up today to be mediocre*

You are NOT here to wait for storms to pass, but to learn to dance in the rain and to live, love and laugh again

CHAPTER 1

The Madness

How did I get here?

It was a weekday, after midnight, and I was locked out of the house in my nighty. Teeth chattering in the cold, I peered through the window at my husband lying flat on his back, snoring like a trooper, and remembering the old saying, 'Let sleeping dogs lie,' I dared not wake him up.

Yes, I was locked out of the house by my very drunk husband, and, sadly, it was very intentional. It would not be the last time this happened, either, as I was about to find out in dramatic fashion.

I was married to a successful man who appeared to have it all: tall, dark and handsome; the gift of the gab, a real smooth talker, who just happened to be drinking a lot and would become aggressive upon getting home. The guilt he felt over whatever he was getting up to elsewhere often caused him to lash out at me, and on this occasion, he woke me up, took me firmly by the arm and led me outside via the patio door.

I had learnt quite early in our marriage not to bother arguing with a drunk man. In fact, I never argued with him at any time by this point, since he was, after all, a very good solicitor who hardly ever lost a case. So, I went along with him quietly, very aware of the possibility that the children would be woken up if I resisted, expecting him to want to show me something by the pool, as he often took a dip to sober up. It was nothing I wasn't used to, until... he stepped back inside, locked the door and walked away, as if he hadn't realised that I was still outside banging on the glass panel. I ran to the front door, hastily stepping on the gravel path barefoot, crying 'Ouch! Ouch!' as the small stones cut into my soft soles, and desperately started to ring the doorbell.

Surely, he can hear me, I thought, but he did not respond.

With my back against the wall, I slithered down to the floor in utter disbelief at the situation; one that would repeat itself on numerous occasions, leaving me locked outside until the cleaner arrived and opened the kitchen door at 6am the following morning.

I had to learn to treat this crazy life as if it was normal, so I became creative in order to survive

One particular night, I slept in a large tree in the garden. I was familiar with climbing trees, as it was something my children loved to do with me, and I used the leaves of the many branches to hide my nakedness. With no phone on me, and no other means of covering myself, I just had to survive the night one hour at a time, glancing down regularly for any signs of movement in the house, hoping that my husband might have had a change of heart.

I had tried standing at the children's bedroom window, calling out their names, but they didn't hear, and it was another long, cold night before the cleaner arrived on the bus and opened the kitchen door. Startled and shocked, she stared at my body, blue from the cold, as I begged her to be quiet and asked if she could run a bath in the spare room, and then bring me any clothes from the laundry – dirty or clean, the warmest she could find – while I ran to check if the children were awake. I attempted to carry on as normal for them, despite how ashamed I was to think that my husband, their father, would do such a thing.

I never confronted him about his behaviour, which only got worse, as I was afraid that doing so would only lead to more extreme consequences the next time he drank.

Not long after the night in the tree, we welcomed a St Bernard puppy named George into our home. Intentionally his kennel was positioned underneath the children's bedroom window, this meant that I got to snuggle up next to him whenever my husband would lock me out again from our house. You would not believe how much body heat that dog gave off, or what a soft pillow he made. I became so inventive, I even put a small blanket, a winter dressing gown and a set of keys (for nights where my husband was able to lock me out again and forget to leave the key in the lock or put the jail across the front and kitchen doors, as was the custom in South Africa, due to regular instances of thieves acquiring copies of people's keys).

One summer evening, my husband was entertaining his estate agents with a pool party, as a way to say thank you for all the conveyancing they had provided. I had realised early on that it was going to be a rough night, when the men and women undressed and skinny-dipping early in the evening, so after ensuring that they had everything they needed food-wise, I took the opportunity to slip away and get into bed, only to be woken up with a fright by one of the male guests. He was standing at the bedside while my husband watched on from the doorway, laughing loudly and saying something along the lines of, 'You two enjoy.'

Bewildered and confused, I asked the man what was going on and why he was in my bedroom. Embarrassed, he somewhat coyly explained that he and my husband had made a bet over whether or not he could get me to have sex with him, and thus my husband had locked us in the bedroom. This man's wife was my partner in the property business, so we knew each other well, and upon seeing the total disgust written all over my face, he quietly suggested that he would just go to sleep, adding feebly that he had had too much to drink anyway. Shocked and now angry at what I had just heard, and without another word, I took the duvet and two pillows, and snuggled up in the bath with the door locked till the next morning.

In order to survive this crazy life, I had to learn to think of it as normal. The pastor nor my friends, had any idea what was happening behind the walls of our very prestigious home. I continued to hold out hope that things would get better, lying to myself that actually I still loved him and blamed all of our issues on the drink.

I was living under the illusion and assumption that things would get better

I had never experienced violence or abuse before, and had no idea that he was an alcoholic. I was blissfully unaware of the dark effects that the 'demon drink' could have on a person, especially somebody I thought I knew.

By day, I dutifully played the role of the happy wife living the good life, telling little white lies to his clients and partners – and, of course, to myself – to cover for all the antics he pulled and trouble he got himself into. I was becoming a person I didn't recognise, compromising my long-held values and sense of integrity just to preserve the façade of a functioning marriage.

BUT I LOVE HIM!, I kept telling myself, and so the journey continued, the *Tears Behind the Smile...*

My Lifelines

- Never be rushed into a decision. In the midst of a storm, the sand is blinding.

- Stop. Breathe. Don't Assume, don't React. The answer will come.

- Learn to Decide, to Discern and to Distract yourself through the chaos.

- Allowing the abuser to shame you only gives him or her the power to define you.

- Never challenge the abuser head-on. Appear to go along with his or her game while you wisely calculate your exit.

- Showing your fear to the abuser only fuels the abuse.

- Distract your abuser in whatever way is fitting, while moving in the opposite direction.

- Never fight back physically unless you are armed with the right weapons.

- Respond in a calm, normal voice, reasoning with the logic needed to disarm the abuser.

- Moving with the opposite attitude softens the blows.

- There are only losers when you fight abuse with abuse.

- Never argue with a drunk person.

- Always have your back-up in place.

- Always keep some form of independence, eg a private bank account or friends that you can call in a time of need.

- If you can't change them, join them, but only if it doesn't mean compromising your own values.

- Get trusted advice when navigating unknown territory.

- Don't compromise your principles in the name of love.

- Be wise and vigilant at all times.

- Embrace truth, and it will bring you wisdom in every given situation.

- If he or she is drunk make sure you are sober, always be vigilant.

CHAPTER 2

It's Not All As It Seems

The honeymoon period ending and reality kicking in is something we all know the possibility of. For me, having come from a secure family background and an old-school conservative upbringing, this was a source of great internal conflict. I was under no illusions about the difficulties of marriage, as being the second-youngest of six girls, I saw the challenges that my older siblings had faced, yet I now found myself questioning my values and everything I knew, in the face of being plunged headlong into my husband's world.

He led a very active social life, and was well-respected in his position as the youngest barrister at the firm he worked for. It wasn't difficult to see why he was thriving in court, as he had all the attributes needed to be a great advocate: charisma, charm and resourcefulness, and he was making a name for himself quite rapidly by building the conveyancing side of the practice, gaining a reputation for finalising a deceased estate in record time. Success was on the cards for both of us, it seemed, both individually and as a couple.

Having two young children and running my own estate agency, a property restoration company, while living in a beautiful, five-bedroom thatched-roof house in an affluent area, you would have thought I had it all. My husband offered me total support as we built business after business together; he bought the repossessed houses, I went into them with my restoration staff, decorating and furnishing for maximum profitability ahead of a sale. The operation ran like a well-oiled machine, and together we were a good a team.

At home, there were wonderful times of total harmony and unity, laughter and fun. We loved each other deeply, and were known in the community as a couple to watch, with even politics thought to be on the horizon. He was a gifted man, and I was steadily growing into a confident businesswoman in my own right.

Blind to the reality of what was really happening

Looking back, I was so blind to the reality of what was really happening to us. It crept in slowly, like a disease, the sense that things did not feel right, but we continued anyway, as we were just two young people who knew how to work and grow together materially. Yes, I grew with him, all the while maintaining the fast pace of the entrepreneurial side of our lives, acutely aware that so many men lose interest in their wives as the couple grow apart, her being a homemaker and him the breadwinner. I knew I had to grow with him, and to begin with at least, I thoroughly enjoyed the journey. That would not be the case for long, though, as the tears behind the smile were already starting to seep through, first as a trickle, and then like a river gushing through my heart, as the abuse increased, and the periods of happiness and family time became less and less frequent. None of this was obvious to anybody else, as I kept denying the reality that things were getting very bad at home. It would mostly happen when I least expected it, seemingly for no apparent reason, as I began to experience strange behaviour that challenged me to my very core.

Finding the wisdom and knowledge to reach a solution that leads to the desired outcome is the ART OF LIVING LIFE

One evening, when we were just going to bed after a whole day of him drinking, he disagreed with something I had said. Next thing I knew, without so much as raising his voice by way of warning, he reached out and grabbed my hair with both hands, one on each side, and began banging my head against the wall again and again, grunting like a wild animal as he did so. It was enough to break the glass frame of a picture of the children hanging on the wall behind us, which you would think would get him to pause, but it didn't, and as the grunting continued, I got a strong whiff of his alcohol breath. He then bent down and picked up a sharp piece of glass, holding it against my neck, close to the jugular vein, while I tried to stand up on my tiptoes to relieve the pressure of the glass piercing my skin, as I felt the blood begin to trickle down.

'Don't hit me – please!'

In that terrifying moment, feeling as though I was going to faint, I grasped his arm in panic and desperation, and caught a glimpse of a pair of eyes that were like those of the devil himself, as the glass was pressed harder against my skin.

'Jesus, help me!' I cried out with a screech. It was all I could muster, a desperate cry for help as my toes could not reach any higher and felt I was fainting.

My neck was being stretched, and I knew this was more than just a drunken treat. Then, as suddenly as it had started, the pressure of the sharp-edged glass was lifted and I was allowed to slide down the wall to the floor. He dropped the glass as if it had just burnt his hand, and in a flash he went from pinning me against the wall to cowering in the far corner of the room with both hands in front of his face, as if protecting himself from something.

'Don't hit me. Don't hit me – please!' he muttered in a quivering voice.

Not even contemplating his plea, I scrambled to my feet and, holding my neck with one hand, ran into the bathroom and locked the door, only unlocking it again after a long period of silence had passed. I moved stealthily across the bedroom floor, where I found him unconscious in the same corner I had left him huddled in. Relieved, and feeling some sense of security in the knowledge that he would not wake up for a good while, I covered him with the duvet and closed the door behind me.

The following morning, he was back to his old self, albeit feeling and looking terrible, unable to make it into work. He had me phone his office with some excuse or other, and I was obviously not going to tell his colleagues what had really happened, nor anybody else for that matter. I then went about my day as normal, despite being tired, confused and badly bruised from the previous night's episode. I had managed to cover the open wound with a scarf around my neck, even though it was summer, but I couldn't stop thinking about the possibility that it might happen again, possibly with more severe consequences.

Meanwhile, he sat quietly subdued in his armchair in the corner of the bedroom, looking at the picture hanging with the one corner of the glass still stuck in the frame.

'Pity I broke our children's picture last night,' he said remorsefully. 'I will have it fixed tomorrow.'

He was always ready to apologise after one of his rampages, and to use his money to reverse the damage, but he could never address the emotional impact of his actions.

Then came the bombshell, as he said in a moment of sober clarity, 'You know, Joké, I don't know why you wanted to hit me.'

'Hit you?' I replied, incredulous. 'If I wanted to hit you, what difference would that make? You are exactly double my weight and six-foot two. Me being five-four, what difference would I make to you?'

'You weren't five-four last night as I experienced it. You were massive, and coming right towards me.'

'Could you see my face?'

'No, but you were huge and it scared me.'

I knew then that I had an angel protecting me, especially when he later agreed that there was something large and bright standing in front of me. I knew God's protection was there, and I became more and more aware of that unseen protection as the abuse continued to escalate.

He continued drinking heavily, but I was not the target for a while, as we were mostly apart throughout the process of building a game farm with seventeen thatched-roof cabanas and a beautiful, massive borehole swimming pool, which was half covered with thatch and featured luxurious seating inside the pool itself. Positioned in the popular Bushveld in South Africa's Northern Transvaal, we named it

Alldays Safaris, and it became a place that my husband used to expand his business influence by inviting clients and potential customers to go on safari. This involved regular drinking binges, but at least it was happening away from me and the children, as we mostly stayed behind. When we did go to the farm, I enjoyed the nature and the outdoor life, especially sitting in front of the mesmerising flames of an open fire. Fresh air, the sounds of nature and the smell of boerewors and lamb chops on the fire; that was the life, even though I had to do all the organising and catering, playing hostess for the weekend. I loved my life, knowing that we had worked hard to build it all from scratch, and eventually creating a Timeshare resort that I would sell through the estate agency managed by my business partner.

I needed to protect my eight-year-old son from seeing what his father was getting up to

We had special times there. The children played outside with local children, building go-karts made of old pram wheels and wooden planks, and taking turns pushing one another through the bushes and sandy banks. I loved to see it, and even joined them several times to the delight of the local children, as they tried try to get me to fall off, the rougher the better.

The game on the farm were used to having people around, like the old giraffe who would peer over at us with interest, as if he knew he was beautiful and wanted our acknowledgment. The deer would trot over to be petted, amusing the guests, but our favourite was a wild warthog who intimidated people by acting like a dog. Imagine, this ugly, wild pig coming to greet unsuspecting newcomers as they arrived.

Sunny, happy family days were spent on the farm, and writing about them makes me long for the Africa experience again. Yes, for sure these were my happiest times. The children would play outside all day, and in the evening, I would bathe them in a tub outside, or just let them go to bed smelling of the smoke from the open fire.

Oh, boy. I was in trouble

On one such trip, I had gone ahead to prepare for some new guests' arrival that evening, joining my husband in our rented bus. I had no idea who would be coming, only that they would most likely be businessmen, as we rarely had women visit, but to my surprise, there were women among them. My initial thought was that this would complicate the sleeping arrangements, but I soon found out that they were escort girls hired for the weekend.

Ugh!

My reaction was less about the girls themselves, and more about the fact that I knew these men had wives back home, many of whom were my friends. Still, keeping my head down, I dutifully prepared dinner as the drinking and party began, after which I would slip away to ensure that the children were protected from seeing where this was obviously heading.

Things got worse as the night progressed, and I knew I needed to get out of there. My son was eight years old at the time, and had enough sense to realise what was going on. I needed to protect him, and not let him see what his father was getting up to, so after wrapping my daughter in a blanket and with my sleepy son in tow, we got into our Trooper van. The children never asked questions, as they were by now quite familiar with Mom doing things that seemed unusual, like moving them quickly in the middle of the night.

Nobody noticed until I started the car.

At first, I thought he must have believed that the van was being stolen, as he appeared in the shadow of darkness, pointing a gun directly at us. Unconcerned, I lowered the widow and called out to him.

'It's okay,' I said, 'it's only me. I'm taking the children to the hotel, as they cannot sleep with all the noise.'

There was no response, and still he kept the gun pointed at us.

I shouted twice more, calling his name in desperation as I tried to spark some sense into my very intoxicated husband, who was obviously not in control of his own logic.

Oh, boy. I was in trouble.

A very, very drunk and agitated man was pointing a gun at the car. The music was loud in the background, as the party was in full swing, and he apparently couldn't hear me until, at last, he came to his senses for a brief moment, and realised it was us.

'You can't go,' he slurred. 'It's too dangerous to drive on the farm road at night.'

It was abuse in another form

'I will be back early tomorrow,' I said calmly, fully aware that speaking to a volatile drunk was unlikely to go well, but seeing no other option.

The gun's barrel was now very close to the car, as my daughter started to wake up and my son stared at me with wide-open, fearful eyes.

Seconds later, live rounds were fired into the van's body, creating the most harrowing sound in the hollow metal as it echoed over the loud music. I will always remember how those shots ricocheted through the otherwise still night as the music was abruptly cut off, while the three of us sat frozen in fear, huddled together in the driver's seat.

Thankfully, some of the more sober guests came outside and took charge as best as they could, or so I was told later. All I remember is that we were pulled out of the car by strong arms, still holding on to one another in shock as we were ushered into the children's bedroom, where we fell asleep totally exhausted and numbed.

Next morning, I was first to rise. I started cleaning up the mess, prioritising the many broken bottles that were a hazard to all of us, as we mostly walked barefoot on the farm. The guests were all sleeping, and though I noticed that my husband was not in our bedroom either, I was too exhausted to care as I went through the motions of setting up breakfast and getting dressed.

Slowly, one by one, the revellers rose and came asking for instructions on how to find and use the bathroom, the facilities being very primitive in this rustic setting. Little else was said as the fresh bushveld air became tinged with an atmosphere of tension, and then one of the guests, who had been outside smoking, rushed inside to ask me where my husband was.

What a rough night you must have had, I thought, eyeing this usually handsome man, who now looked a haggard mess.

'I don't know,' I said. 'He was not in our bedroom when I looked this morning.'

The bullet holes were right round the petrol tank

Outside, two other men were looking intently at the van, rubbing their hands over the multiple bullet holes in its body. To everyone's astonishment – it must have been a miracle – the bullets had only just missed the spare petrol tank, forming a pattern around it. That was when they realised that my husband very nearly blew up his own family without even knowing it, as the bullets were mere millimetres from the tank.

Once again, it seemed I had been protected by a supernatural force; there was no other way to explain it. Silence hung in the air, flabbergasting all who saw it, as the story soon reached the local news and even the mainstream newspapers.

Following this rude awaking, the party broke up and the guests took themselves home that same day, leaving my husband so shocked at what might have been that he never invited business guests to the farm ever again. Either that, or they themselves were not comfortable at the thought of entering this crazy, out-of-control environment.

This led to weeks of sobriety, but then, just as I was letting my guard down, he went off on a binge again, only this time without involving his friends or family. These types of binges, which involved him not coming home for a week at a time, brought their own challenges, but at least neither I nor the children were exposed to what I came to understand was abuse in another form. Thus, I continued on with tears behind my smile, as I tried to make sense of what I could possibly do to salvage my marriage.

Divorce was not an option.

My lifelines:

- Worry does not empty tomorrow of its sorrow, but it does empty today of its strength.

- Whenever you find yourself in a storm, take time to be still, to let the dust of your mind settle, and the answers that show you the way out will come.

- Finding a way forward requires honesty. The reality, and then the answer to moving on, will follow.

- Dare to feel the pain. Embrace it, and allow yourself to cry. It is not a sign of weakness, but a sign of your inner strength.

- Your silence is a time to build your knowing of the What, the When and the How, remembering that there are potentially three types of people in your life:

  i.   *Who helped you in difficult times?*
  ii. *Who left you in difficult times?*
  iii. *Who put you in difficult times?*

Choose wisely!

Difficult times may lead
to beautiful destinations.

CHAPTER 3

The Demon Drink

*Dancing to an impossible tune that has
no rhythm of truth, love or hope to it*

The look in his eyes, the constant uncertainly of wondering what next, the fear of confronting him when I knew I was in danger, constantly trying to make sense of what was happening, even when I knew he was in the wrong.

My life was mostly spent walking on eggshells, and it was getting worse.

My father was a non-drinker. As a family growing up, we never had any alcohol in the house, so both it and its consequences were alien to us. Thus, when I realised that I had married an alcoholic, I found myself knee-deep in frightening unfamiliarity.

Dancing the dance of acceptance and denial

Looking back, my upbringing could well be described as a sheltered life. All being well and plain-sailing were my default experiences, which only added to the shock of being thrust into the world of alcohol misuse and the subtle abuse that comes with it.

The rapid escalation from occasional drinking at weekends could not have been predicted, nor could the effect that it would have not only on my life, but also the lives of my children, as well as my other immediate family and business partners. Like any addiction, the **Demon Drink** creeps up slowly, and bearing in mind that in those days there was no such thing as Google, or even the internet, it was much more difficult to get the information and advice that I was so desperately in need of. I felt so alone, and was often desperate for advice and understanding about what was happening to us as a family. I found I was forever questioning myself, as I carefully asked around while trying to air my thoughts and feelings, all the while being conscious of not undermining or compromising my husband. Between the persistent internal conflict I had regarding his drinking, and the endless questions about the abuse that was happening, I was exhausted.

I tried covering up for him by making excuses, even to my own family, and looking back now, I can't believe I was naïve enough to think that nobody had noticed there was a problem. I just hoped that the issues would somehow resolve themselves, and went on believing it must have all been my fault, as I considered the possibility that my enduring faith was the actual fuel feeding this fire.

The following years became pure hell, as I danced the dance of acceptance and denial. He had a drinking problem, and so much unacceptable behaviour was not only happening, but getting progressively worse, as he became so arrogant that he started acting as if he was above the law, using his legal knowledge to intimidate law officials and anybody else that dared challenge him over his drunken escapades.

Manipulation and charisma got him out of many situations, as I started getting calls at all hours of the day and night, summoning me to fetch him from various places where he'd been locked up or became stuck, and several times even from the hospital. His sharp decline was only made all the more conspicuous by the injuries he was suffering, such as a fractured jaw (got into a fight with a bouncer), crushed knuckles (punched the roof of the rugby tour bus) or the effects of driving headlong into a ditch or fence on the farm. Still, I dutifully (or maybe just fearfully) picked him up, and even nursed him, but when I finally found the courage to start implementing a tough-love approach, the abuse really began to escalate in my direction. There were times where I feared for my life, resulting in me lying face-down under the bed on the cold tiled floor most of the day, as he ranted and raged in the house around me, breaking everything that I valued and spent time nurturing, like my potted plants and vegetable garden. It was forcing me to choose my plans for each day according to his drinking habits, at a time where I not only had to keep my business going, but was also responsible for keeping the children out of harm's way. I felt something like a soldier in the midst of battle, constantly on high alert.

Love denial

My husband drinking at home became the norm, and all I could do was wait for a few moments of silence that would give me hope that he had finally passed out. Then, if the coast was clear, I would sneak out to check if he was okay, as crazy though it may seem, I was worried about him hurting himself; the nursing side of me rising up to the surface.

The fear was so intense that it was obvious to others, but not to me. I was in a love denial.

I would pay the bills, but I stopped putting the whole cheque in the bank from his source of income, which enabled him to buy his friends drinks at the bar. I also stopped nagging him and did not accompany him to parties, as his behaviour was always excessive and embarrassing, humiliating and hurtful for me to continually be exposed to. I became detached and numb to the abuse, and thus blind to the escalation, by continuing to try, hoping and praying that this time he had reached rock bottom and would have no choice but to confront his issues. However, he did not seek recovery, instead finding new enablers. This left me incredibly sad, as I danced to an impossible tune that had no rhythm of truth, love or hope to it.

We began to exist in silence, living separate lives, yet remaining together as the word 'divorce' was never to be spoken. Remarkably, I was gaining strength, as I become acutely aware of how all this was affecting my children, having accepted that I simply could not protect them from the truth any longer.

On a summer Friday afternoon, he arrived home in a rush, stating he was taking the children – our son was five years old at the time, our daughter just three – to a hot springs resort called Warmbaths for the weekend. My immediate thought was that he would not be able to protect the children from drowning, as he would be drinking while chatting up every woman around him (this became an obsession for him whenever the drink started to flow).

'How will you look after the children?' I asked, slightly irritated.

His response was to point to the car outside, where, looking out, I saw a strange woman sitting in the front passenger seat, giving me a sheepish wave.

Mixed messages flashed through my mind.

What is my husband doing going away for the weekend with another woman, and who is she exactly? I wondered, before a more practical thought appeared. *At least a woman will be with them, and she'll able to protect my children. That's what women do, right?*

Thinking on my feet, so to speak, I realised his determination, as he was already on a drinking spree. That meant his driving would be another issue to consider, so I went out to the car and, with my utmost composure and intention, I spoke to the woman, introducing myself and asking her name. At this point, I didn't even care who she was or what she and my husband were getting up to. My focus was solely on appealing to any maternal instincts she might have had, as I asked her to please look after my babies, and to watch them closely around the pool as neither could swim. This was the basis of the conversation, as I fought to hide my emotions under the stress of knowing that I would have no control over my children's safety. She nodded and gave a faint nervous grin or smile, and though I was still unsure about her true intentions, she was my only hope and lifeline in this situation.

With the pain and anguish of a mother's heart, I passed out

Thirty minutes later, I bit my tongue as they left with two excited children, who innocently thought they were going swimming with Daddy. I held back my tears as I realised that my worst fear was playing out in front of me, and I could not do anything about it. Up to that point, my children had always been under my protection, and it was knowing this that allowed me to handle the physical abuse without protest. Now, however, the extreme alert buttons were being pushed, and the sense of hopelessness and powerlessness were overwhelming, as I dropped to the floor at the sight of the car speeding off. Screaming with the fear, pain and anguish of a mother's heart – alone, exhausted and exasperated – I passed out face-down on the cold, black slate floor.

Finding myself on the patio floor, I came to with tears pouring down my face. I called on God to protect my babies, and asked Him to give this strange women (who I later found out was a hired escort girl) to love my children and to look after them, especially around the pool, as they both had no water sense and needed water wings and a constant eye on them. My faith and fears were being tested to the maximum, as we reached the stage where my husband was not only failing to take care of his children, but was now an active danger to them. I felt betrayed, and I also blamed myself for betraying the trust of my children by meekly letting them go off into such a potentially dangerous situation. Even to this day, I could cry at the memory of that feeling of utter hopelessness, but what else could I have done? It would have been traumatising for them to witness a tug of war between their parents, and would ultimately have only made things worse. I had to choose my battles wisely, even when the correct choice was also the most difficult to stomach.

Thankfully, as quickly as the ordeal had started, it ended as early as the following morning. My husband was home before ten, with two, smoky-smelling (from the barbecue), scraggly-hair and tired, but completely unharmed, children in the back of the car.

Embracing them in pure relief, I didn't even dare to ask why they were back so soon, as I was just so relieved. Apparently, for whatever unknown reason, the escort lady had been very adamant about getting them home in good time.

A mother's prayers had been answered!

I finally realised that I was no longer able to protect myself or my children

Checking outside, I peered around to see if the escort was still in the car, and after seeing no sign of her, and watching my husband skulk off to bed, I decided it was best to say nothing more on the matter. Privately, however, I was rocked by the realisation that the situation had escalated such that I was not able to protect myself or my children, with only the grace of God to thank for the fact that nothing had happened this time. Yes, the binge cycle was only winding down for the moment, and the next one would be along soon enough, with new tests and challenges to face, but at that moment, I was simply happy to have a bit of peace and normality for a few days. I fully embraced it, understanding that this was as good as life as I knew it could get.

Without the proper support needed, I was struggling to find the strength to break the chain, limiting myself to praying and trusting it would happen soon. It was so hard, and I still wish he would have agreed to get help. I prayed every day for the solution that would turn everything around, naively believing that love alone was powerful enough to fix our broken marriage. Then came the moment when my son's teacher in a private meeting asked if everything was okay at home, before explaining that he was showing signs of stress and abnormal behaviour at school, forcing me to face the reality that my inaction was having a detrimental effect on my children's development. At once, the decision was made to move out of the house before any lasting damage could be done, and focus switched to planning our escape.

Silently planning my escape

The very first night after I made my decision, he somehow cottoned on to the change in me. Alcoholics are usually very intelligent people, and I knew my husband was gifted in so many ways. One of his talents was for playing chess, and it's fair to say that he checkmated me several times.

No sooner had I heard the devastating news from my son's teacher than the shenanigans started again, and I had no choice but to park with my sleeping children in a cramped Ford Mustang just out of view of the house. He couldn't see us, but I could still see him, as he set about throwing out my clothes and bags onto the front lawn. Then, to my surprise and horror, he took my prized possession, an old grandfather clock, and shot it till it fell over and shattered into pieces, before walking around shooting the flowerpots on the front porch, till the early hours of the morning.

Amazingly, none of the neighbours called the police or even came out to check what was happening.

The devil does look after his own, I thought, although I never had the nerve to call them myself, either. I'd have been too embarrassed.

I was saddened to think that my grandfather clock would no longer wake us up with it melodious chimes, and while that may seem like a shallow response on the face of it, I knew the message he was trying to send by destroying everything I valued. It was the demon drink at work, and I was obviously the victim playing to its tune, but then wisdom and confidence started coming into play, and I started silently planning the details of my escape. I had finally found the inner strength, having resolved to take my children away from this craziness once and for all, with as little fuss and confusion as possible.

Being gentle as a dove, cunning as a serpent, I thought.

What a growth challenge that was!

With a determined single-mindedness, and without discussing my plan with anybody else, I waited until he passed out and immediately started packing necessities and stashing them in the shed. I then took all the cash I had saved, and filled the Mercedes ready to go the next morning while he was out at work. He was oblivious to the drastic move I was preparing to make, never in his wildest dreams believing that I was capable of doing something so bold. I didn't even tell the children what was happening until it came time to load up the car, as even though I could have trusted my son to say nothing, I knew it would be too much for them to bear. Plus, I knew it was only the element of surprise that was protecting me from getting caught.

So, off we went to start our new life, going where nobody would find us and leaving no hint of our planned destination (this was long before cell phones with track-and-trace apps), and not even telling my close friends or sisters, as I knew he would try to intimidate them with his legal lingo.

Yes, the great escape was in action, as I covered – or at least I thought I had – all potential avenues he might have had for finding me. We were heading directly for the coast, to a town a thousand miles away called Port Elisabeth, and my children could sense the relief, freedom and excitement that I was exuding. They didn't need much of an explanation, either; they were just happy to be going on an adventure. I told them what they needed to know and answered their questions, noting how they never asked why Daddy was not coming with us, probably because they had become accustomed to not having him around.

Port Elisabeth is a beautiful coastal town, and I had secured a position as a nurse in a mansion home on the beach front, caring for a middle-aged woman who was battling cancer. I enrolled my son at the local school and put my daughter in a crèche (a preschool), and the three of us lived in a room attached to the house with its own bathroom. There we spent three precious and peaceful months, during which time my smile started coming through oh so briefly.

That night, he raped me twice

Everything was going so well. We were creating our new normal as we settled down with surprising ease, considering we had only the one room and the bare minimum of toys, with no luxuries at all to speak of. We were content and very creative in making the most of what little we had, until suddenly I found myself facing a police officer questioning me at the mansion's wide, barn-like swivel door. He politely asked who owned the Mercedes outside, and when I told him I did and I had the papers to prove it, I noticed somebody hiding behind a large shrub to the side of the door.

A chill ran down my spine, as I knew instinctively who it was.

With a victorious, arrogant stride, my husband stepped out from behind the shrub.

'Hello Joké,' he smirked.

I couldn't believe it. He had found me.

The police officer explained that I had no right to take the Mercedes, and as I tried to explain that it was registered in my name, my husband used legal jargon to convince him that he had still legal possession due to the fact that it had officially been paid for by his company. Once again, he had misused his persuasive powers to get what he wanted, leaving me dumbstruck and helpless.

Here we go again, I thought, realising that after losing this round, he would do all he could at whatever expense to get me back home, which was exactly what happened.

Choose your battles wisely!

He had me hastily pack our belongings in black bags while he impatiently hovered over me, watching my every move and not allowing me to call anybody or even go to collect our toiletries from the bathroom. Then, without so much as saying goodbye to the household, let alone explain what was going on, he roughly ushered me into my Mercedes and drove off to pick up the children, leaving me guilt-ridden at abandoning these lovely people and the sick lady I had been looking after.

On the journey home, I concentrated on games of I Spy with the children, as I attempted to keep the atmosphere as positive as possible. I could see that they were baffled by the whole experience, but I just continued to prompt them with games to break the tension until we stopped at a motel for the night.

The room was cold and very basic, with a double bed and a converted veranda where the children's bunkbeds were placed, thankfully sparing them from witnessing what was about to happen.

I tried to resist, but he insisted that he was claiming his marital right, and then he repeated the act twice, as though the first time he had not been enough to leave me demoralised and conquered. There was less resistance the second and third times, as he claimed me back like an animal establishing its dominance.

The tears behind the smile were flowing, as the long journey home went on.

My Lifelines

- Never argue with somebody who believes their own lies.

- It doesn't matter if it's a relationship or a job.
  If it doesn't make you happy, let it go.

- Don't allow somebody to treat you poorly just because
  you love them – or you *think* you love them.

- Predators make you believe you're a bad person so that
  they don't feel guilty about the things they do to you.

- Once somebody avoids you, don't disturb
  them again by pushing their buttons.

- Never fight a wrong with a wrong, as nobody wins.

- I know I always have the Power to Choose, the Power of Letting
  Go and the ability to step into the Power of my Now.

- Choose your battles.

- Get to know the enemy by letting them think they are the
  victor, giving them enough rope to hang themselves.

- Always stay calm when threatened.

- Your fear only fuels their will to terrorise you.

- Put your mind in another space when they are
  violating you, remembering that they are encouraged
  to be more violent when they sense fear.

- If somebody rapes you, don't dwell on it.
  This gives them power over you.

- What he or she did was violate your body, but NOT your soul.

- Try to detach yourself from your body while it is
  happening, as this will protect your soul.

- Look after your soul by controlling what you let in wherever possible.

- Always remember, this is just a brief moment in your life. You
  don't have to relive it or let it overshadow the rest of your life.

CHAPTER 4

Prisoner of Love In My Own Home

O n the journey home from Port Elisabeth, the palpable atmosphere was only subdued by our shared desire to not let the children notice what was truly happening. The stop-offs to overindulge the children with treats and gifts, playing on their little minds by being the cool dad, had me cringing at the falseness of it all, but I was not able to protest or even mildly disagree, as this would risk escalating the abuse in full view of our son and daughter. Ultimately, it was easier to join in, and maybe part of me even enjoyed this reuniting of the family unit, albeit briefly and with no shortage of guilt.

Forgetting the pain and embracing the now

Arriving home and seeing the luxurious house I had left behind, I couldn't help but feel happy as thoughts and flickers of hope ran through my mind, like small streams of light filtering through the dark clouds of the cold, harsh reality. I was glad to be home and so were the children. They immediately called their friends and had a reunion in the pool, just like old times, bringing smiles to mine and my husband's faces, as the previous night's rapes were forgotten.

I went inside to unpack, and he went out of his way to support me as I settled back in. The little bit of normality was bliss.

It's amazing how one adjusts to an atmosphere or situation automatically, briefly forgetting the pain and embracing the now. I didn't know for sure if it was the right thing to do, but I had to choose my battles wisely as I planned my next escape attempt. I was living in a minefield, and the only way to successfully navigate it was by keeping my cards close to my chest.

I asked him if Sophie, my house help, was around. He did not answer, so I just assumed he must have given her the weekend off, but as I unpacked the children's things, I found their toy box in shambles, with puzzle pieces, Lego blocks and dolls' clothes all scattered about their room. I then noticed a child's shoe amongst the Lego, and upon closer inspection of this tiny pretty sandal, I realised it was not my daughter's. My heart pounded with the knowledge that my personal space had been violated, as I contemplated the fact that another child had obviously been playing there while her mother was in my house doing whatever with my husband. All kinds of upsetting images were rushing through my mind as I welled up with emotion, unable to digest it all as I unpacked my underwear and found items that didn't belong to me in my drawers. At that point, I flipped out, addressing my husband while holding up a pair of leopard-print G-string knickers along with the child's sandal.

'Enough,' I said. 'No way am I accepting this.'

It was the worst thing I could have done, as it only fuelled the fire of his guilt, and from that day on, things took a dramatic turn for the worse.

The paranoia began

He had somehow unsettled Sophie such that she quit her job, costing me a loyal friend who had worked for us for years. He disconnected the telephone, cutting off all contact with the outside world, and arranged for his secretary to take the children to school and pick them up again, in addition to doing all my shopping, undermining me as a wife, a mother and a woman. It was no surprise when I found out that she also had an affair with my husband, which only made me feel even more ashamed and worthless, but I dared not speak to her about anything anyway, as I could not trust anyone. I could only wonder if she was the one who took my nighty and who had a little daughter whose sandal I found.

The paranoia began, as nothing made sense through all the shame and disbelief I was finding myself in. He wanted to control me totally. He wanted both me and the freedom to do whatever he wanted, flashing his money around and utilising his charm, charisma and knack for calculated manipulation. He had it all going for him while I was just the wife at home, doing the cleaning and cooking in the prison that was my own house.

To keep myself occupied, I cleaned the house till it was spotless, and I also maintained the luscious garden and fine lawn, trimming and nurturing conifers of all shapes and sizes. Meanwhile, my daughter had her large doll house fully furnished, and my son received a Pug 50 cc motorbike that became a welcome family distraction. We all enjoyed riding it, even though it ruined the lawn. I even made a stepladder to hide between the shrubs, which allowed us to pop over to the neighbours' garden for the children to play, and for me to seek the human contact I so desperately needed. The lady next door clearly knew more than she let on, but I never said much since her husband and my husband were not only friends, but worked at the same firm.

Yes, I was lonely, but I found ways to keep myself busy, and he generally left me alone while he was off on binges. I at least had my spotless home, and since maintaining it was all I could do, I did it well, making the best of the situation by trying to find an outlet, as divorce was still not the answer at this stage.

Toilet-time reading

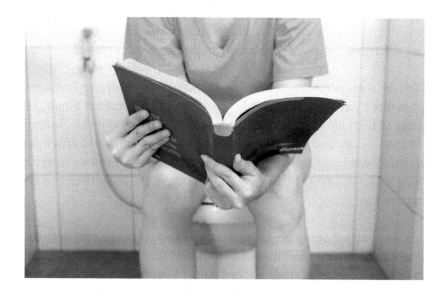

My family were getting more and more concerned, so he allowed me to speak to them from his office while he listened in the background. I was grateful for small mercies, and having plenty of time to contemplate my situation, I started self-analysing as I looked for answers to my dilemma. I found much-needed privacy in reading self-help books and my Bible, which I hid in the guest bathroom book rack, knowing full well that he never went in there. Slowly, I started to increase my knowledge and personal growth, rediscovering myself and finding the courage to face my reality as never before. I became acutely aware that if I didn't change myself, my situation wouldn't change, as I started seeing everything around me with a fresh prospective. These were my first steps in the right direction, learning that knowledge is power and being empowered brings understanding. I was not allowing the situation to break me. I knew it was only a passing season, and as I learned more lessons and found more answers, I started to truly believe that I would win.

It may be a cliché, but it's true that whatever does not kill you makes you stronger. I am living proof, as I am stronger for this experience.

Had I lost myself?

My smile returned gradually, even though my circumstances were very unusual. I found consolation in toilet-time reading, making it my sacred space (I'm sure God didn't mind the venue, LOL). Soon enough, my whole countenance changed, which didn't go unnoticed by my husband. I was becoming bolder in my silence, smiling on the inside, and this was making him curious. I was also teaching my children to recognise that their dad was an alcoholic, describing it as a sickness that comes and goes. Of course, that isn't exactly correct, but it was a good way to explain the time he would spend recovering in bed after a week-long binge. They started recognising the difference between their father being 'sick' and when he was not drinking, knowing when they could relax and enjoy the kind, nice person he was without the influence of the 'Demon Drink'. Becoming wise beyond their years, they learned to walk on eggshells when needed, managing to lead normal lives while making the most of a daddy who would give them all the things money could buy, as the three of us found ways to survive together.

Truthfully, I was in denial, but it was easier to relish moments of peace and the financial security. As a result, I was losing touch with myself by compromising my core values for fear of getting a divorce and becoming financially vulnerable.

What a copout that was!

I had replaced one lie for another, and had to lose myself to live with it.

During that period of submitting to the situation, I had learned to mother my husband. Every time he had an accident, I nursed him, even feeding him liquidated food through a straw when he had his jaw wired together. I was there for him, despite it all being self-inflicted through the demon drink.

One time, after he fell down the stairs, he feebly asked me to help him up. Now, considering I was half his weight and could hardly lift him, even with all my nursing training, I could not get him up; he was a deadweight.

'Get up,' I said loudly from the top of the stairs. 'You got there yourself, so get yourself up.'

It was so hard for me to stand up for myself, and to fight the urge to help him, but I was growing my resilience muscle by exercising tough love.

Eventually, he got up and mumbled his way down the passage to the bed and fell asleep, which felt like a small victory and a step in the right direction, as I was able to go to bed myself, ready for another day of imprisonment in my own home.

Just as I felt I was making progress, he unrepentantly announced that he had sold the house; my very clean house, which had become a safe haven for me. I was finally getting used to the hiding and the isolation of living in my own thoughts and feelings, but there was no discussion and no consideration for how I thought or felt.

Half the furniture that I had so lovingly collected throughout the years was included in the deal, with complete disregard for the value I had attached to it.

There goes my false security, I thought.

Meanwhile, the binging continued, but he was now staying away for weeks at the time, and my phone was reconnected, purely out of convenience for him to get me to sort out the move. I also got my car keys back, as the preceding three months of isolation and no communication with anyone, gave way to a month of me being on a mission to organise our surprise evacuation. This brought new challenges and new lessons to learn, but these contributed to my steadily growing resilience and ability to standing on my own two feet.

I have been sleeping with your husband for a while now

Then, only days before we were due to leave, Cynthia, a good friend of mine came to visit, which was quite unusual, and she seemed a bit uneasy whilst I served tea and scones.

'We are very old friends,' I said to her. 'Nothing you say will shock me, so out with it.'

She blurted out her reply as if it had been burning inside her like food poisoning.

'I have been sleeping with your husband for a while now, and I cannot keep it a secret from you any longer.'

Though stunned at what I had just heard, I couldn't help but notice her show signs of relief. I could not get a word out; the shock of what she had just said was too much to comprehend. She was a school friend who I'd known for donkey's years, and now she was telling me this.

What, where and how long were the first questions that came to mind, before it struck me that a year ago, I advised her to use my husband as her divorce attorney, which must have been when it started.

She was very willing to offload all the gory details about how supportive he was by sending her flowers, telling me what a good man he was and how much she respected him.

All the while, I still couldn't get a word out. My head was spinning as I tried to absorb what I was hearing until, finally, I muttered a response.

'Why are you telling me this, Cynthia?' I asked.

She continued to blabber on and on, not even hearing me. Then, a second blow hit me like a cannonball to the gut, leaving me breathless and faint, too painful to withstand. She said she wanted to tell me because she had found out that he had several other women besides her, which made her feel betrayed.

The irony of it all was too much. I couldn't hear any more, and I asked her to leave immediately. I knew now I had to get out of the messy marriage, but where would I go?

Amazingly, she seemed surprised at my reaction. It was as if she wanted to talk it through as friends, even though she had betrayed our friendship and my trust to the maximum. I knew that either she had gone insane or I had, but whatever the case, I calmly ushered her to her car without any hint of reaction beyond the look of horror and disbelief etched on my face. I needed to be alone to digest what had just happened, and to compose myself before he came home.

Now she is the victim!

I was so dismayed. It was as if she had wanted me to condone him only having one other woman in his life, even going so far as to point out that I had introduced her to him in the first place. I was only doing what any friend would, but now she was somehow the victim. It was total craziness what I was hearing from her, and what an incredible, unbelievable twist she put on it to suggest that she was the victim. What right did she have to even think that after having an affair with *my* husband, especially when she was supposed to be my friend?

I never spoke to Cynthia again. There was no need, as I had enough on my plate between the moving and the balancing of a very fragile marriage.

In hindsight, I realise I learnt a big lesson that day. Cynthia was the person who I had confided in the most, telling her my deepest feelings and fears, as we had practically grown up together. However, by exposing my deep secrets regarding my marriage, and with her going through a divorce, I had unwittingly laid the groundwork that led to her betrayal. She knew exactly what kind of friend I was, and because I was so used to forgiving my husband, she assumed I would forgive her, too. This experience also taught me that blind trust can be dangerous, and will often lead to you setting yourself up for hurt, failure and disappointment. That's what happened here. I gave her a lifeline, and in doing so created a scenario that brought about the end of a lifelong friendship.

Yes forgiveness was done (for me as she never needed to know) it was time for intuition and wisdom to assert themselves, as my naïve, trusting nature was getting me nowhere. I needed to grow up, and fast. For my children's sake as much as my own.

The move went ahead, justified as a way to raise the money needed for the safari farm, which my husband tried to convince me as a fresh start. He said he would not have as much pressure at work, so he would be at the office less and less, and that I would have a share of the profits. He also promised that there would be no more cheating, since he would be on the farm working most of the time.

Did I believe him? Yes. Hope springs eternal, and I was desperate for what he said to be true, that he had got to the end of himself and now things could be different. I did love him, at least in terms of what I understood to be love at the time. He was my first love, and I was still growing up. Even if I was experienced in business, I was a novice when it came to the life lessons I was being forced to take.

The Tears behind the smile had dried up for the moment, as I forgave him once again.

My lifelines:

- This is not what defines me, so I will not let it in.

- Find the Lie, the Truth and the Choice.

- Be still in the storm, silence your heart.
  Breathe, and your answers will come.

- Never react to the abuser with words, but with
  calmness and composure. He or she is merely an
  intimidator waiting for a fearful response.

- Don't fuel the fire of your abuser. Fires only escalate and turn wild.

- Trauma teaches you to close your heart. However, healing teaches
  you to open your heart and learn to put boundaries in place.

- Feel the pain, embrace it for a moment. Forgive
  yourself, and then forgive the inflictor and let go.

JOKÉ HOETMER

CHAPTER 5

Young Love —
My Children's Father

At this stage in this book, after reading the chapter *A Prisoner of Love in My Own Home*, I feel it is important to point out that how the marriage ended was not how it started.

There are possibly so many couples today, married and in partnerships, who will identify with the initial attraction I had to George. It all started so well; we were just two young people in love, with great potential and possibilities for our futures. When we first met, he was studying Theology and Law with such ease, and with his charismatic personality, his good looks and his influence and success in business, he appeared to have all the makings of a real winner. As the young admiring bride bringing up my baby boy and girl, I had so much love and respect for him, and having completed nursing training and qualified with honours, before going on to work in various different private hospitals and gathering lots of experience, I was determined to be more than average in my field.

I just *knew* I was destined for more than that.

The love we shared in those early days was full of laughter, adventure, excitement and hope. Nothing could stop us fulfilling our maximum potential, as we grew into our reputation as the golden couple of the time.

If only I had known the pain, the suffering, the challenges, the heartache and the destruction that was to follow.

Looking back, it was all about choices: the choices he made, and the choices I made. The choices we made.

As his father once said to me: *'You are praying too much, and he is drinking too much.'*

And wasn't that the truth.

As he made his way towards becoming a well-respected, successful attorney and businessman, I retreated deeper and deeper into the solace of looking for answers. I saw the cracks appearing, but I had no idea how to circumvent them, since having grown up in such a protected family environment, I was still so very naïve. Our foundations were so very different, which was reflected in our contrasting reactions to success and failure. I had no idea what I was up against, or how to deal with the life I was experiencing, as I unknowingly set off on a journey to discover the truth of my life, pursuing all the previously unanswered questions:

- What was going on?
- What was the reason for it?
- Why was it happening to me?

The biggest and most bitter pill to swallow was betrayal

It took me five years to accept that he was an alcoholic, and then the following decade was spent being consumed by a hell comprised of destruction, distortion, confusion, violence and abuse; the by-products and inevitable results of his alcohol abuse.

However, the biggest and most bitter pill to swallow were his betrayals.

The betrayals with women and with finances; the betrayal of hope. The lies and deceit that confused me, as well as so many others who truly loved him for his larger-than-life personality and knowledge, which he used not for good, but to have a particular desired effect.

For many years, I had been busy rebuilding mine and my children's lives with no contact from George, and then in August 2019, completely out of the blue, he contacted me and we spoke again as if nothing had happened. Time had no right to claim the destruction that had accumulated within our family, not when it had caused so much pain, like a bushfire consuming everything in its way, but he was crying and asking for forgiveness, saying it had been tormenting his soul, and I shared with him that I had already forgiven him a very long time ago, he just didn't know it.

He was so relieved and surprised, and we had such a good conversation. It was beautiful. It was amazing, as if no time had passed, even though he said I sounded like an English lady, which we had a good laugh about.

Looking back, I think of the destruction and chaos that his choices and his drinking caused, and how I tried to stay the course all throughout, wanting to always do the right thing, to speak the truth, to love unconditionally, to keep the balance, to survive the ordeal and to heal the pain.

In the end, he lost everything. He died without his children around him or even knowing his grandchildren. He died without experiencing the truly happy and strong family we now are. I, on the other hand, have two beautiful, righteous children and three grandchildren, and for that I am grateful.

Both his children have their father's intellect, strength and his tenacity. I am grateful for that, too.

On our wedding day, a golden couple

Without George, I would not have my beautiful children, and my experiences while married to him taught me not fear any man or anything else for that matter. Unbeknownst to him, in the time since we parted, forgiving was always in the foreground as I worked to move on from the pain of the father of my children.

When I received the news that George had died peacefully, with a good countenance on his face and not in pain, I was relieved. I also cried.

Perhaps it was a release of long-held sadness of the trail of destruction, a journey perhaps of, could haves, should haves.

JOKÉ HOETMER

CHAPTER 6

Mind Games (the Battleground)

My mind became so indoctrinated and filled with the wrong, I reached the stage where I couldn't remember what was right

S elf-doubt was overwhelming me. I became totally confused about what I believed to be right or wrong, and I was losing myself in the process.

This was the hardest part of my journey to self-discovery and growth. The innocence and security of my childhood had not prepared me for the battlefield I now found myself on. I was not equipped to face this challenge at all, and I intuitively knew that something had to change.

Self-doubt and shame, even to the point of blaming myself for his problems

I reached the point of consciousness and total awareness that it was me who needed to change in order to find wisdom and the survival skills to master emotions and thought patterns that were based on fear, self-doubt and shame, even to the point of blaming myself for his problems. I had to learn to unpick the lies he was telling me and to see the games he was playing with my feelings, all of which was a journey on its own.

Having no support from the onset, nor even being able to tell myself the truth of the matter, my initial response had been to try ducking the arrows of the accusations that I repeatedly allowed myself to ponder on, as I wallowed in self-doubt on my own internal battlefield.

Externally, the war was being fought on two fronts. The first being my young children, whose safety was my primary concern. The second was the marriage itself, which required me to walk on eggshells and not rock the boat, as this would only make things worse.

What I really needed to do was seek professional advice, and to surround myself with much-needed support givers, but I had no idea how to make this happen.

It was the shame of the lie I was living

More than anything else, it was the shame of the lie I was living that prevented me from seeking the support I needed, and so instead of sharing my distress with a friend or family member, I covered it up by always dressing well and making sure there was a smile permanently plastered across my face. Even so, the lie was obvious to those close to me, who were able to see right through the façade of my automatic 'I am okay, thanks' answer to their enquiries.

Physically, I was suffering with shingles and IBS, in addition to exhibiting regular memory blockages, whereby I just couldn't remember how to spell a basic word or forgot what day of the week it was, or even forgot my own birthday. There were also numerous occasions where I started driving somewhere I knew the way to and ended up getting lost.

Many a time, I was tempted to drown my feelings with the readily available alcohol, just to ease the pain or to let me sleep for a few hours. However, I never did give in to temptation, knowing that it would have only brought temporary relief. I didn't dare take calming or sleeping tablets, either, as this would mean letting my guard down and becoming even more vulnerable than I already was. It is said that an alcoholic will pull five others down with them, and I can see why it might look like the easier path at certain point, but through grace and strength, I never went down that road myself.

Dying without seeing his children or grandchildren

Despite my best intentions, there were still moments where I did let my guard down, such as when I attended functions where I ended up being very out of sorts and visibly uncomfortable as the only sober person present. This would typically end with me driving my husband home in the early hours of the morning, and then rising early to get the children ready for school and myself to work, whilst he stayed in bed recovering.

I did actually enjoy being around his friends, at least until we reached the stage in the night where the drinking got out of hand, and I found myself being embarrassed by my husband's unpredictable and sometime violent behaviour towards the authorities or his companions. It was a no-win situation with no end in sight, except the hope that this time he would hit rock bottom and have no other option but to commit to rehab. It never happened, though, albeit there were times he appeared to come close.

All the while, my mind was still lingering on the battlefield. The damage done had left scars, and now even the truth was continually overshadowed by the pain and discord I was facing daily, as I was confronted by internal questions about what I should or could have done differently to save my marriage. He was my first love after all, and a marriage should last forever, right? That's what I'd expected in the fairy tale-like beginning, before the duelling feelings of love and pain, hope and hopelessness took hold, compounded by pure exasperation at not wanting to give up.

Unfortunately, this was a war of attrition that would continue until the bitter end when, three months before he died, he finally made his breakthrough. Regrettably, this didn't come soon enough for him to see his children or to meet his grandchildren. The **demon drink** had claimed that part of his life for good, and very nearly took mine and my children's with it, as it left an indelible mark on their most precious formative years.

CHAPTER 7

The Blame Game

Inviting Blame Into My Home

Always my fault, of course

As the years progressed, the pressures mounted, and without knowing it, I had invited blame into my home. Everything was always my fault, of course. All the situations and the predicaments that we as a family found ourselves in.

Accusations were just part of the blame game, as he looked for ways to soothe his guilt over not being at home to support us. I was blamed for not being a better wife and mother. I should have been more prudent, which was laughable, seeing as though I was the main source of income and he controlled our budget, which he frittered away. And yet he constantly passed the blame on, all the while absolving himself of responsibility for the calamity he caused.

The blame game would get quite complex and convoluted, as he played the victim despite his problems being obviously self-inflicted, leaving me, the true victim, to bear the brunt for whatever went wrong.

> *By shifting the focus to who made the mistake which led to the problem, the blame game distracts people from why the problem occurred in the first place.*

It's all just a game, though; one that makes it hard to discern right from wrong or good from bad, not to mention truth from lies. I was being bombarded by this very intelligent man, who knew how to fight psychological battles with verbal intimidation, which resulted in self-doubt about who or what I was, never mind what I could possibly be doing to stop this endless whirlwind that I found myself in.

There were few and far between moments where things seemed to settle down a little bit, and the storm looked to have passed, but I eventually learned to use these as opportunities to prepare myself for the next storm, knowing it would likely be even worse than the one we'd just had.

The ongoing mind games and abuse were at the forefront of my thoughts as I went about my day, the questions always being: *Did those bad expectations contaminate my mind, and is what's happening now the result of my projecting?*

I had to admit that a lot of what I thought could happen ended up coming about, as if I had manifested it. My mind was playing its own tricks on me, so after realising that I was over-analysing, I decided I just needed to be careful what I was dwelling on, especially the expectation part. This is difficult to do when one has been abused, and I found it easier to take the blame in order to keep the peace, saying sorry even when I did not feel I was guilty. As a result, I was basically redefining myself according to his image of me.

However, after taking a step back, and with much rehearsal, trial and error, I started to apply the *Art of War* to my own particular circumstances.

In divorce, there are no winners

Even though I got divorced more than once, it never became easier. In fact, it was harder, as the self-blame became more intense. I began to see myself as the obvious common denominator, and thus shouldered all the guilt and shame for us having failed to keep our vows. It was like a dress code that I was forced to wear, even if I didn't want or deserve to, because I must be this man-hating bad wife. I would constantly compare my own situation to the successful marriages my friends had, before reaching the inevitable conclusion that there was something inherently wrong with me.

Naturally, invitations to dinner parties and functions dried up, as perhaps my friends thought that now I was single, their husbands could be tempted to give me unwanted attention. All unnecessary as far as I was concerned, but exhausting nevertheless. This led to me also disinviting myself at times, which only caused even more pain and reduced self-worth.

Odd lady out

The stigma of being a divorcee in those days was quite severe. I was no longer welcome at my children's school events, especially rugby matches and wrestling competitions, which my son loved, as I was now the odd lady out. Even when people found out the true reasons behind the breakdown of my marriage, the perceived stigma never went away. The arrows just kept coming, and I kept letting them hit me.

Worse still, the loneliness and isolation I was experiencing was filtering through to my children, as they were also forced to carry the burden of shame for being the products of a failed marriage. My son even began to blame himself for being unable to protect his mother.

Ouch! That was a hard one to hear.

Having once been overindulged, the children now had to adjust to a much more basic lifestyle, due to my chronic lack of funds, which, combined with a distinct lack of fatherly guidance, saddled them with insecurities that were an added source of stress for them and guilt for me.

Counteracting the blame and shame scenario

Finding ways to live and love our lives again without a husband and father, and in particular the abundance of money and security he offered, was a journey of choice. I chose to survive and to make things right by letting go of the losses and what ifs, could haves and should haves, instead embracing a new now.

Challenging the single parenthood and blended family

Each and every week, we held a family meeting on Sunday evenings. The TV was turned off, snacks were put on the table and we settled down for some family time. The first time we did it, their faces said it all. They were obviously expecting some kind of reprimand or rule-setting, despite me stating that this was not my intention. Thus, it was hard to get the conversations going or to get them to open up, due in part to the various age gaps between my children (by this time, I had five teenagers all from different backgrounds, living as a blended family), but these meetings eventually became a lifeline for bringing strength and unity to our fatherless family. It was run something like a business meeting, discussing our respective schedules and planning the week ahead.

The real success of these family meetings was how it created a platform for open conversations on any topic that was on their minds, starting with me being the example, and then each one of them having their time to share their likes or dislikes about what I was doing. I was open to suggestions on how I could improve, giving them an outlet for their individual frustrations or issues in the process.

I found myself in the firing line the first few times, as all their various grievances hit me like a ton of bricks. However, I resolved to embrace their outpourings with total respect, asking what they would do differently and respecting their opinion. At times, I was merely setting myself up to be the family punch bag, with five teenagers all aiming blows, but while I would certainly feel the hits, I also earned their trust by making changes wherever possible, thereby setting an example in regard to the benefits of listening and respecting others' views.

We were a family again

We also established family rules, which were designed to teach them to give and demand respect no matter what, regardless of how seemingly trivial a particular issue may appear. Nobody was allowed to ridicule anybody else or be deliberately hurtful, and it was through this that we reunited as a family again.

I always knew what was going on, and had a good sense of where they were at mentally and emotionally. It was also a bonding time, as we were able to be vulnerable with one another, and it soon became the highlight of the week for the whole family, filled with honesty and integrity, laugher and love, as we strived to live by our family motto 'Stick together, no matter what,' which still drives our relationship to this day.

It gave me great satisfaction to see the meetings more than serve their purpose as they became the backbone of our survival, training and equipping us to go out into the world and face life's challenges.

That was our collective success, and on a personal level, I had reached a point where I no longer obsessed over convincing my husband or anybody else of my value. I knew the truth, and I was going to walk in it.

My Lifelines

- Don't play the blame game, as the game will
  never finish and nobody will ever win.

- Allowing him or her to shame and blame you for everything
  is you giving them residence in your house.

- Tit for tat only makes you the loser, as you
  have stooped to the abuser's level.

- Believe in your self and celebrate the small changes.

- Remember to forgive yourself and laugh at yourself.

- Intentionally chose to do things that make you happy.

- Don't feel guilty if you are happy again.

- Choose to dwell on the lesson and not the pain.

- Be mindful of the smile you are expressing, that it is
  genuinely true to how you are feeling, it is like your
  thermometer to check the state of your heart.

- Trust yourself as you learn and embrace the new you.

- Blaming yourself, drags you down, praising
  yourself for the small steps is the answer.

- **Remember to be able to laugh at yourself, it takes away the blame and shame.**

- **Mostly forgive yourself as you are all you have.**

CHAPTER 8

Finding the Voice That I Never Knew I Had Lost

Not having a voice in a relationship can be catastrophic. It implies that what you feel doesn't matter to him or her, which begs the question why are you together? Having no voice in a marriage leads to a fear-based energy driving your actions, making it almost impossible for love to flourish.

Keeping quiet about your personal suffering is a crisis waiting to happen, and in my case, as the lack of transparency and communication became more and more apparent, I found I was not able to speak and articulate my true feelings. It started off with me being quiet, as I thought it was not important enough for them to hear, especially if it meant rocking the boat and potentially causing more conflict.

What I didn't realise was that this was me setting the whole worsening scenario in motion.

The fact that I was violated for several years from the age of three had been buried deep in my subconscious mind, where it remained hidden until I was fifty-five. The ramifications and effects of this past abuse came through in my lack of foundational boundaries, and the confusion that coloured much of my life.

If a father, an uncle or a teacher (or any authority figure for that matter) sexually abuses a child, its personal boundaries are violated, causing a perversion of truth that will reverberate throughout their whole life. For this reason, it is perhaps worth considering that a person you know who apparently has no boundaries might have suffered some form of abuse themselves.

A child instantly knows that what's happening is not right, but only questions the abuse temporarily. Eventually, when everything has returned to normal, the experience embeds itself deep in the soul, where it festers into guilt and secrecy.

My mother was not aware that such a thing was even possible, never mind that it could happen to her daughter

Growing up as one of six girls, I always knew my relationship with my dad was different from those that he had with my sisters. He gave me more attention, and overindulged me in whatever ways he could.

For a short period in my childhood, I was aware that I had developed a keen interest in my own sexuality, which went beyond the normal curiosity that a child would have at such an age. As a twelve-year-old, I opened up to my mother about a family friend being inappropriate towards me in ways that suggested clear sexual intent, only to be gently brushed aside, as she was not aware that such a thing was even possible, never mind that it could happen to her daughter. Meanwhile, several other instances occurred with older men, including an English teacher who tried to kiss me. Here, a pattern was being formed, but once again, when I attempted to discuss it with my mother, nothing was done.

Slowly, I began to believe that I was the problem, and the notion that my voice was insignificant became an intrinsic part of my identity. Later in life, I could never open up to my husbands, as I never felt emotionally safe enough, hence the obsession throughout my life with not being protected.

I had lost connection with myself, as my values proved to carry no significance in the real world.

Suffering in silence became more intense until it was eventually a default setting

In an argument, I would always back down and be the first to say sorry, even if I hadn't done anything wrong. At the time, apologising seemed to be a way for me to take the high road and diffuse a situation, but the reality is that I was reinforcing the belief that my opinion carried no value. Not knowing how to verbalise my real needs, suffering in silence became more intense until it was eventually a default setting, foremost amongst my unhealthy coping mechanisms. Having locked away a traumatic past, I had succeeded only in kicking the can down the road until I was mature and conscious enough to face the trauma head-on.

The silent suffering was raging within me. I knew this wasn't how life was supposed to be, but crafting my life around trying to avoid certain feelings was becoming exhausting. The lie became a way of life that took away my power to truly be me, causing yet more tears behind my smile.

I began to ask myself if it was my beliefs and self-inflicted mind traps that had led me towards an unfulfilling life of constant abuse, hence my constant seeking of a fulfilling relationship through my marriages? Was I seeking the impossible dream of a life that so many other couples seemed to have, but was not destined for me?

> *The choices I made, fuelled by the fear of not being protected, caused my husbands to be the very thing I feared, and in the end, I needed to be protected from them.*

Nobody has a voice in this type of relationship

I had learned to live with my internal battles, normalising myself to a limiting existence, but I never gave myself the time to search for the answers. Working hard was my means of avoidance, and it was only when l started counselling abused woman and children that I discovered my own truth through the research I was doing to help them.

Numbed at the result of my overwhelming battle to stop my detachment blocks by allowing myself to become vulnerable enough to create a healthy connection with others, my identity was based on avoiding my fears, unaware that this would only lead to smaller thinking that kept me down, and I thus became far less than my true potential. I am sure my husbands were aware of this, and that it confused their natural tendency to protect me, with the balance of a healthy relationship being doomed from the start by my not letting this happen. Perhaps they felt unloved and had their own battles to fight, but whatever the case, I was clearly the common denominator, and so I had to find my path to healing.

Nobody has a voice in this type of relationship. It affects everything from communication to sex life, making intimacy impossible as there is no healthy connection in place. The reality was that my silence and calmness were huge signs of my emotional detachment, which would lead to me feeling numbed and incapable of expressing anything other than resentment.

I had no option but to put my energies elsewhere, be it my work, my children or the adopted children I had living with me, as these pursuits became my only sources of identity and fulfilment. The relationship patterns had become obvious, as I recognised that by trying so hard to save a marriage, I was turning myself into a hamster on a spinning wheel.

I always used to say, 'When I stop crying, that is when I know it's over,' which was my way of trying to communicate that we needed help. I would tell myself that everything would work out and get better in the end, as long as I looked after myself and the children, who were always my first priority. 'This too shall pass,' I'd insist, as I sought counsel from those I trusted. 'I know I am worthy of so much more. I know I am stronger than this. I can beat this if I understand the how, and believe with all my heart that the best is yet to come.'

Hope kept me going, but it was the truth I was seeking, as I knew that it alone could set me free.

> *Conscience is your inner voice that guides you, so speak it out boldly, it will liberate you in your truth.*

Lifelines

- Not having a voice in a marriage means that a fear-based energy is directing the relationship. This makes it almost impossible for love to survive and thrive.

- You can't grow love while you're worrying about protecting yourself from your partner.

- I am not broken. I have just experienced life negatively.

- Life can sometimes suck, but you should never be a sucker.

- I have a mind, a will and emotions. I also know right from wrong, so therefore I have a choice.

- Don't hide your true self, as you never know who is looking for help from exactly who you are.

- Always make sure you are heard, and always hear your children out.

> *There are no right or wrong feelings.*
> *Whatever you feel is okay,*
> *and you have a right to express it.*

CHAPTER 9

Inner Conflict

'But I love him!'

The question I kept asking myself was, do I love him more than I love myself? If so, it must mean I had no self-love, as I was allowing myself to be abused in all different ways.

What the heck does self-love mean anyway? I wondered. *Is it not conceited to love yourself? What do I really want from this relationship if all I care about is being loved, heard and understood?*

Respect and truth are my two highest values, so I had to ask why I was tolerating going without either. Other couples seemed to have these things in abundance, so I knew I was missing something.

Change is never easy

I began to wonder if I even deserved to be in a loving relationship, as I spent years trying to understand how my husbands had all abused me in their own ways. Being the common denominator as the thread of abuse showed up every time, I felt it was up to me to find the solutions that would stop this cycle repeating itself. However, finding the solution is only the first step. Having the guts to implement it is where things get difficult, as change is never easy.

Despite my confusion, what I did know was that I did not want this, whatever 'this' was, for the rest of my life. I had to figure out exactly what it was that I was holding on to. Was it financial security, social status (for the children's sake as much as my own) or the fear of being alone? What could I have done differently to remedy the way we were living, and what were the options if I could not change him? To join him in his pursuit of destruction, accepting the impact of drugs, alcohol and continual lying and betrayal, going tit for tat until the bitter end?

No way!

At the end of the day, laying all the cards on the table, is anything worth being unhappy, unfulfilled, undermined and, possibly, in line for further abuse? I arrived at the point where at the end of the road was a decision that I and I alone had to make. Enough was enough, action had to be taken. Putting up with the status quo was no longer an option.

I had to do the inner work to get the outer results manifested.

Perfection doesn't exist

Ouch, I finally stopped striving to be the perfect wife and mother. I learned that self-love is vital in overcoming past painful memories and healing inner wounds. Self-love helps us to understand that it is human to err. It helps overcome any guilt or grudges we may be carrying that have prevented our inner wounds from healing. Self-love is the ultimate medicine to heal those inner wounds. It helps you to forgive and move on, so I vowed to start developing it at once, and to experience happiness and security inwardly instead of searching for a man to provide them, reasoning that this is how we love being as children.

I came to fully understand how affairs happen, as one can easily be driven to it, though I never allowed it to become an option for me, despite having several opportunities on my journey to find myself in. Love and praise are rewards we receive when we do good things as children, and perhaps we never grow out of this, as we continue to seek the same things as adults. However, the love we are really looking for can only come from within. Somebody else's love will never be enough for us to be truly happy, and I believe we can never feel safe and secure until we are comfortable with our own capabilities and confident in loving ourselves.

After discovering the practise of self-love, I was able to push through my limiting beliefs and live a life that was truly rewarding. I took a deep breath, gave myself a little hug in front of a mirror – yes, and why not – it was my breakthrough after all – and started living by the following guidelines:

Who says you have to be perfect?

Want the perfect body, perfect family life and well-rounded children? Truth is, perfection doesn't exist. It's all fabricated to fit the imagined ideals that we buy into. Now, what a relief to be able to make mistakes and move on. Yep, and I sure did make those mistakes, but who is counting, no one, as I was my own worst critic.

Don't live according to other people's expectations

I was always unhappy because I would want more, which led to me comparing what I had with an unrealistic standard that I thought I could see in others. This was only leading me to lack self-worth and perhaps put me on the verge of depression and never being happy or satisfied even when things were good.

Living in the Moment

I took moments to stop the endless pursuit of happiness and just soul searched, and surprised myself with what came up. It exposed where I had come from, and allowed me to start appreciating the beauty of the moment, the fun I had with my children, the unconditional love I received from my dogs and my general health. Yes, I was alive, a living, breathing, functioning woman, and what a luxury that truly is, slowly becoming my reality. As I embraced it with my arms wide open, yes, and my childlikeness was coming to the foreground again, this time much wiser and conscious.

Being grateful

Perhaps when I became comfortable, I actually became ungrateful. So, I had to change my position to start showing gratitude every day in all situations. Intentionally displaying gratitude was now my key. In the beginning, it was challenging to find several aspects of my life that I needed to be grateful for, but I persisted until I found a way to stop looking at my life through dark glasses and embraced hope.

You can't control everything

I learned to understand that I can't control other people, their choices or their behaviour (being controlled by his bad behaviour, didn't mean that me being in control of my mind, will and emotions, was bad, but a good thing). I could then, however, learn to control my own responses, knowing that the situations will work themselves out eventually, and learning to only be responsible for my own actions instead of being accountable for his actions and choices. Bam! I finally got it!

Self-Care
Subconsciously, I felt that self-care was selfish. Perhaps my greatest fear was to be labelled selfish, especially as a mother, so I worked and performed to be perceived as good in whatever I was doing at the cost of my happiness, and ended up losing myself in the process.

Check in with yourself emotionally
I took a deep breath and asked myself, *How are you feeling?* I didn't just brush the answer under the rug to be dealt with later, either. I had to constantly be mindful of my true emotions. That was hard at the beginning, but became easier as I adjusted to my recovery.

Facing your negative thoughts
Ask yourself, are they true? Are they helpful? Are they kind? If anything negative comes up, I ask if it benefits me in any way – does it make me better in some way – or is it just confusing and belittling me? Really getting to know myself, it's like looking in the mirror and seeing all the flaws I have, but then embracing them kindly and lovingly as I say to the world, 'This is me, and I am comfortable with that.'

Separate the truth from the lie
I realised I could be mentally abusive towards myself. One of the most important keys to happiness is to stop the internal torture, as my thoughts became my beliefs and my beliefs became my reality. My internal chatter had to become more positive, with any negative thoughts being captured and corrected through being still, mindful and prayer.

In time, self-love became the building blocks of setting up the power to say 'No!' to abuse, as I finally stepped into the real me.

Never compare yourself to others

Not to your peer group or any other personalities, as everybody is unique and faces their own challenges in life. Just being you is always the best path and more than good enough. Your strength comes not from exploiting the tactics and brute force you have experienced, but from having the courage to endure without becoming somebody else's pain.

Your mind is a powerful thing. When you fill it with positive thoughts, your life will start to change

---

Regular exercises I practised to love myself, by standing in front of the mirror saying out loud:

- 'I am sorry!'
- 'I thank you!'
- 'I forgive you!'
- 'I love you!'

I continued these exercises daily, even though it felt weird and made me laugh and feel ridiculous at first. I persevered, as I knew it was the beginning of loving myself, not him.

Lifelines

- If it isn't the right puzzle piece, why try to force it?

- Letting go takes courage.

- Becoming my own best friend was a priceless gift to myself.

- Letting every situation be what it is, instead of what I thought it should be.

- I started to concentrate on what I loved and liked about myself, and kept reminding myself of my many strengths.

JOKÉ HOETMER

CHAPTER 10

The Casualties of War

The Family, the Children and Friends

Looking back at my journey – the ups and downs and the bad decisions – the effects it had on my children were ongoing, as were the unnoticed wounds and pain suffered by family and close friends who stood by me throughout my rollercoaster ride of abuse. Of course, the children were being affected the most, a fact that really showed its ugly head as the years went on, teaching me to never underestimate the influence that your emotional wellbeing has on your children, who will soak it all up like little sponges, learning how to grow up by observing their parents. Children silently absorb the habits and lies as if they are normal aspects of life, and I had to work relentlessly to restore a healthy family dynamic before the damage done to them became irreversible.

I felt I had failed them by allowing their early lives to be defined by the abuse I suffered, and I was racked with guilt over not having the answers to protect them. This was the strongest driving force behind me finally changing and taking drastic action. My main priority was giving them as much stability as possible during the tumultuous times, whilst also maintaining open dialogue with them (on a need-to-know basis, of course). I never tried to get them involved in adult problems, nor did I ever diminish their father or vent my own frustrations in front of them. Well, I at least *tried* not to, but I could not always stop them from seeing their mother stressed or crying.

Children are so perceptive, and I tried to mitigate this by being as open as I could about my pain without going into too much detail, showing and sharing how I was overcoming that pain and learning lessons from it. This was a gem in my relationship with my children, as I believe that if a parent is seen purely as an infallible authority figure, the children will very quickly realise when things are really wrong and may lose respect. I found that by being open and transparent with my children – never blaming their father, but seeking answers together – I encouraged their input and helped them to understand what they were witnessing. It also worked both ways, as their perception and feelings were so informative to me regarding how they were coping. Plus, they were often a source of practical solutions, which helped prepare them to master their feelings and emotions such that they always knew right from wrong.

'Mommy, I [pro]tect you!'

One time, back when my son was barely able to talk, I was trying to muffle my crying in the pillow whilst lying face-down alone on my bed. He climbed on the bed with his little green plastic water pistol and said, 'Mommy, I tect you!' (in his baby language, disguised as a little man).

He was mimicking his father, who always kept a gun under his pillow when we were on the bushveld farm. He couldn't speak properly, but he already had a sense of being a little man that wanted to protect me. So sweet! It made the tears flow even more, but with joy this time, as I witnessed the early signs of a protective instinct that he maintains to this day.

It was an image that remained in the foreground of my mind: the big, brown-eyed baby boy, barely out of nappies, displaying the little man who was already there inside him. From then on, I started treating him like the little man he was, respecting his views – usually much to my amusement, as the words that come out of babes is often honest and funny at the same time – and valuing his input, even to the point that at the age of seventy-two, I got my future husband to ask him for permission to propose to me. So weird, when the mother becomes the child!

I took something that was traumatic for a child to see whilst growing up and used it to develop a balanced young adult, a man in his own right, who is now a loving father in a happy marriage. He realised he had a choice between good and evil, and he chose good.

Which side of the coin do you choose, heads or tails?

Whenever my children had to make a choice, I encouraged them to choose heads or tails. This didn't mean tossing the coin, but rather using it as a focal point in the choices they made. Heads meant good and tails was bad; heads symbolised the power and self-respect of identity, whereas tails was the loss of positive things such as self-respect, voice and hope.

The Head   The Tail

However, despite all my efforts to protect my son, there was still lasting damage beyond my control that lingered right through until he was in his late forties. It was a continuous work in progress, and we stayed close with a very open and balanced relationship, able to discuss anything, even very personal things, including vulnerabilities and fears.

Luckily, my daughter was spared much of her father's abuse because she was so young. However, at a later stage in her adolescence, she still had to intentionally go through the process of healing and letting go of the abuse she saw. Her faith and her stable, mature, loving husband had a lot to do with her healing, as they allowed her to go through her journey with the wisdom and protection she needed. Today, she is a beautiful, pure, well-grounded mentor, revered and loved by all. A dedicated mother of two talented boys, she also juggles the counselling of many woman and teenagers with her profound wisdom and power. Until today we can speak openly and learn for each other as she took the batten off me, as her counselling and wisdom astounds me. With great gratitude I see how all the destruction turned out for good.

Our Pain turned into our Gain!

I discovered the right balance with my children. They were always encouraged to be part of any decision I was making or had made. As painful though it was, we were in it together and always stuck together as a family, even when I added the foster children and we became a blended family, welcoming two 'orphans' who I am still supporting today.

In an effort to create an open environment in which it was okay and safe to share their feelings, I regularly asked my children as they showed signs of distress or sadness, the following questions:

'Tell me what happened?'

'How did this make you feel?'

'What are your thoughts about what should be done?'

'How can I help you feel better or make things right?'

'Tell me more?' (repeat until I feel they have got to the point of what the real issue is.)

'Who else but us has been affected?'

'What needs to happen in order to move forward as a family?'

Each one of my children needed to be heard and understood, and seen to be exactly where they were. It became apparent that they were also feeling guilt over matters that in real terms were not of their making (as I had a blended family, they all had different aspects of pain and ways of dealing with it). The anger and resentment developed throughout lives that had been turned upside down turned to self-loathing and disrespect, even going as far as self-harming, as the rejection felt after losing their father made them turn inwards, causing mood swings and temper tantrums that were obviously results of the inner conflict of an absentee father. They blamed themselves for their father leaving, which was very hard for me as a mother to see.

Meanwhile, I was constantly questioning myself, asking how I could address these circumstances whilst working three jobs to maintain the wellbeing of my family (in total, I had eight children in and out of the family, all having their individual challenges and temperaments). I was both mother and father, trying to ensure the children led as normal lives as they could, making sure that laughter could be part of this painful and emotional rollercoaster.

Having five teenagers of both sexes and close in age was a challenge of balancing hormones and monthly cycles with the girls, which required educating the boys to never ague with a girl at certain times as they could never win. The boys, with their fragile egos, were growing up and had started dating, with the younger girls watching and giggling, embarrassing them, and then, later, walking in their nighties in front of their so-called brothers, not realising the effect it would have on them. It was challenging, however despite everything, they were now living as brothers and sisters.

It was a challenge to educate them, especially as a single mother working long hours, and to be able to keep a watchful eye on these situations. Thankfully, my true and trustful house help was another pair of eyes in this crazy blended family scenario, and all was good as we managed and they grew up. They were putting the rules in place themselves, just as I had taught them, and set about ensuring that they were implemented, but with each child interpreting things differently, it still wasn't easy being a single mum. Finding the balance between discipline and love, whilst also teaching them how to become well-balanced adults, was always my aim, as I strived to ensure that the kids wouldn't be negatively impacted by the abuse they saw. They could also sense tension and strife, so even if they don't see you being abused, they can still be negatively affected by the violence they *know* is happening.

Not having much time to myself to study, research or seek counsel, I had to use the only mode of survival available to me: my faith. Thus, I utilised quick prayers to find the answers and request the wisdom to handle situations correctly, becoming a sort of pray-as-you-go mother. Growing my 'faith muscles' was difficult, as I was too ashamed to expose myself to well-meaning counsel about what was continuing to happen to me. It was ridiculous in my eyes, so what would somebody else think?

Eventually, isolation turned to self-condemnation, as I took it all on my shoulders and was very hard on myself, as if I needed to be punished. Drugs, alcohol or even prescribed drugs were not an option, as the children were growing up fast and I needed to be an example as much as I could, and so hanging on to my faith would have to be my way through and out of the immediate situation. The hope was that things would somehow change of their own accord, and in my darkest hours, as I looked for the wisdom to find answers, my faith never failed me as I remembered that I had always found growth on all fronts.

Can abused children become abusive parents?

Too young to do, too naive to understand or stand against it. Knowing what happens to an open wound, as it's a nice target for another time, if there is an unhealed hurt, I will go out of my way, unconsciously, and get hurt in the same spot again. It is bound to happen.

That's what happens to the trauma that people like me have. It never heals, and keeps attracting more trauma in different forms. Thus, the question became, would my children follow in my footsteps?

My focus was not so much on myself as on the effects of what my children were experiencing, as I tried to protect them as much as possible. Whilst they were young, it was easier, but as they grew older and became more active participants on the journey, no matter how much I tried to protect them by getting a divorce from one alcoholic father, only to then step right back into it with another father who was a misogynist, followed by another who played mind games and controlled subtly, squeezing the very life out of us, to the point that the damage continued showing up in some of my children in different ways.

My biological children, as well my two children from my second husband, have grown up to be wonderful fathers and mothers, and no abuse has been transferred to their children. However, I fostered and then adopted two others, as well as my third husband's son, and I could not say the same about them. As these children were teenagers or over the age of nine by the time they came into my life, the abusive foundation had been laid in their formative years, and when damage is done so deep, the anger, resentment and paranoia continues. The rejection and shame wrapped up in being alone and abandoned, which led to them rejecting their own children, is still present today for one of them, and as a family, we support them as much as we are allowed to.

> *'I have never met a single woman who has not faced trauma—child sexual abuse, rape, discrimination through verbal / psychological abuse, early sexualisation, emotional manipulation, and the most common: public grabbing. It's an umbrella term for being forced into doing something that you are uncomfortable with, you know is wrong or are forced to do.' – Unknown*

Each child responds differently to abuse and trauma. Some children are more resilient, and others more sensitive

I learned that there are two kinds of people when it comes to a wound. The first kind make sure they never get hurt again, and heal well later, but the second kind just keep going back to the wound.

Each child responds differently to abuse and trauma. Some children are more resilient, and others are more sensitive. How successful a child is at recovering from abuse or trauma depends on the following:

- a good support system or good relationships with trusted adults
- creating high self-esteem by encouraging them for the little steps in the right direction
- praising them with 'well done' and unconditional love
- never talking down at them, but reaching out, even if I had to kneel to be on their level to have the eye contact and bodily connection
- to connect to where they are at, and not as an adult to a child.

We developed healthy communication on their terms, and I didn't display shock even when they came out with things that shocked me to my very core. Learning to have a poker face helps when, as I experienced first-hand, teenagers like to shock you or try to provoke a reaction. Sometimes, I provoked them into screaming and hitting the pillow to get rid of their frustration and anger. It worked, allowing them to release their frustration physically, as they learned healthy ways to deal with their emotions and memories as they matured. Occasionally, I had to hold them tight in a loving embrace, and be silent and persistent in the holding till they accepted the love and security they so badly needed. One of my adopted daughters – at the time nineteen, taller than me and slightly lighter – was in this love embrace, sitting on my lap, very uncomfortable and odd to see. However, as I continued to hold her, she started to relax and then, finally, she put her arms around my neck and stayed there till I knew she had totally released. That was the first time she had had any physical contact with me in the form of a hug or embrace. It was amazing, a major breakthrough, and we still have this bond of love and acceptance today. She was my wild child, and now she's an example to all the other children, a total turn around.

The sooner a child gets help, the better for his or her chances of becoming a mentally and physically healthy adult. I tried as much as I could, getting youth counsellors, teachers and friends of mine to help. We used to swap our teenage children for a few days at a time, as they were all of a similar age, building up their trust in my friend and me, and letting the teenagers share their feelings. Thus, getting advice from somebody outside the families worked. Sending them to youth camps and on hikes really worked wonders, too, as there were always professional mentors on the teams. I would befriend these mentors informally, and then subtly give a bit of background on my child, so that they were hopefully encouraged to 'see' them properly. All done with my utmost charm and delivered as a plea for help me. Me being a single mum, it always worked.

A mother will do anything she has to for her children, right?

The keys are helping them feel safe, talking to them about their fears and letting them know that it's not their fault (also, fault-finding is not the answer). By talking about what healthy relationships are and are not, they will know what to look for when they start romantic relationships of their own.

I believe it's a side effect of not being able to properly process the trauma. Is it because of self-blame that unprocessed trauma leads to a lot of resentment, especially towards the rules that let the trauma happen in the first place? I was the parent that had to protect my children and I could not, as I was a victim of my various abuses as well.

I HAD BROKEN THE FORMAT OF A GOOD MOTHER.

It might not have been sexual or always obvious, as I was a big mama bear ready to protect them, but as a young adults, my sons experienced unfairness and biased discipline from their stepfathers. They were respectful sons, but not always dealt with fairly by their stepfathers, building up an underlying resentment and anger that can remain deeply hidden till much later in their lives. I am aware of the battles that are still there in myself and my children's lives, patiently waiting for the opportune time when it needs to be addressed and healed. Therefore, it never surprises me when the conversation turns up with the pain showing, but we manage to address it there and then, without fuss or judgement, so we can move on.

This has been ongoing until now. The respect and love we have for one another allows us to be open and to resolve the issues either way. Sometimes, the children help me using whatever I taught them, and I gladly take counsel from them, often with a good laugh at the end. Having a healthy balance between facing the pain and utilising healthy methods of dealing with emotions and memories is the mature way to go about it.

Laughter nearly always follows the pain.

It was only through this open relationship I had with my children, and their own determination to not be like their dads, that we were able to fight this. Thankfully, none of them married abusive spouses, and now the cycle has been broken. The two last and youngest foster care / adopted children are still in the process of healing, and my faith, hope and support remains with them. One can only help if the subject themselves are prepared to do the work, however, as we are all responsible for our own outcome in our lives.

I never brought my children into the marital conflict, nor did I undermine my ex-husbands in front of them. After all, they were their fathers, and I made sure they did not have to take sides.

My Lifelines

- Seize the moment to address the situation.

- Use every situation as a tool to connect.

- Give as much age-appropriate information as possible.

- Give children the option to choose.

- Allow them to express how they feel.

- By exploring your pain with the honesty and the respect needed, so you can resolve the pain gradually.

- Love conquers all.

- Allow them to dream, as well as to spend time to be quiet.

- It's all about balance between holding on and letting go.

- We were never alone, as I believed in my higher self of God in me.

- It's not what happens *to* you that defines you, but rather what happens *through* you.

- Step into your true power and destiny.

- We all have the CHOICE.

- Equip your children and teach them the way to go and grow.

- Don't over protect them from life's happening, as this is a way for children to develop their character and resilience for their future.

- Never speak down or at them. Speak their language, so that they understand you.

- It's not what you leave your children that makes them great, it's what you leave *in* them.

- Being the best example you can be, is perhaps the best way to teach them right from wrong.

- Try to respect their views and feelings, as that's the art of change.

- Sometimes it's not your opinion that matters, its their need to be seen and heard in their pain.

JOKÉ HOETMER

CHAPTER 11

Who is Holding the Remote?

W hen a frog is put into lukewarm water, he will happily swim around. Put him in hot water, however, and he will jump out.

This made me think of the warning signs I should have seen long before I married them. Hindsight is a wonderful science, not to mention a sad fact of growth, and my need to be a submissive wife instead of laying down boundaries at the beginning of relationships is very much like the frog story. The warning signs and red flags were not as clear as I would have thought, leaving me to wonder how it is possible that I gave the remote control of my life to my husbands, allowing them to lead me in directions I would regret in so many ways?

The father of my children was a dynamic, articulate and intelligent man, who quickly rose to become the youngest partner in his legal firm. Charisma and charm enveloped the super intelligence and cunning savvy that could be swung either way, good or bad, and he had great convincing and agentive abilities, which saw him promoted and respected by his peers and colleagues alike. I was in awe of him, I was in love. A young love that accepted all and gave all.

Growing up with an old-fashioned religious belief that I needed to be submissive, I did not know where my personal boundaries were, and like the frog being oblivious to the ever-warming water, I just didn't see it. By this time, I was earning an above-average income through the various properties I sold, supplemented by a house décor business, which involved doing a 'makeover' of repossessed properties that my husband had access to through his conveyancing with the building societies. The money I made was placed in a separate account to which he had signing rights, the arrangement being that he would put in some working capital whilst I renovated and sold the property with the help of a team of agents. The legal transfer of ownership was done by my husband, and so the associated bank balance grew to a substantial amount.

At first, this went very well. We were a great team, as he never got involved in the day-to-day running. Eventually, however, he started to use this account to turn the farm he inherited into a safari lodge, selling me the dream that this represented a bright future for us, as he would no longer be office-bound. As a result, he got more involved in my business, in his desperation to maximise the financial income in order to be set free to realise his ambition of running this farm. This meant I had less and less control, and ultimately no decision-making powers, over a business that had been based entirely on my way of doing things. Up till then, it was working well. I was good at negotiations, and especially at the décor part, having put together a team of freelance artisans to support me, but he wanted contracts and negotiated stringent deals, which made me uncomfortable on many occasions. The final word was always his, and I slowly lost the team due to his business style being so different, taking away the team spirit that always delivered a job well done, and replacing it with satisfactory job done to his standard.

Slowly but surely, the business came to a standstill, and the safari project, which I was initially on board with, became a place where he would host his drinking binges and corporate do's. Thus, seven years of building a successful cash flow through my 'side-line business' (as he called it) came to a halt.

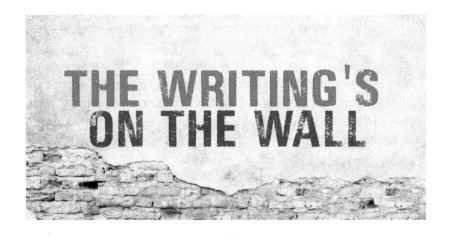

THE WRITING'S ON THE WALL

Why could I not see the writing on the wall? I blindly trusted him, letting myself believe that he knew better, as I was in awe of his superior education and highly-specialised knowledge. Here, the lies regarding my value and significance started trickling in, like the water beginning to heat the frog, as my perspective was pushed to the side by his overpowering techniques of persuasion, which were enough to convince an Eskimo to make a standing order for ice. Subsequently, any good advice I got from family and friends was disregarded, as I gave in to the lie that he was the boss, the man, the head of the household, and thus the final say was his.

That was my default. Not the truth of the value that I brought to the business, or the natural talent I had for this line of work, especially when it came to establishing a bond with my staff, being both a leader and a team player as we got the job done with great satisfaction for all involved.

In my personal life, I was giving him more and more power over my day-to-day activities, not wanting to oppose him for fear of getting the wrong reaction, which was happening on an increasingly regular basis anyway. Soon, it was fear that controlled my actions as things got tougher at home, and slowly but surely, I abandoned my true self in order to appease him. I was no longer a wife, I was merely a doormat.

He showed neither respect nor love for me, making it clear that my feelings had no value.

Who had I become? The tears were now permanently behind the smile, as I constantly feared the inevitable moment when the physical abuse would start again, compounding the ongoing emotional abuse I was facing.

I was drowning, but what could I do? How could I get out of this pit?

Worse still, even when I did escape, I ended up repeating the same mistakes with my second husband!

Right motive, wrong decision

After divorcing my first husband, I married a man who had no material assets, but had wriggled his way into my life through my children, who were so desperate to have a father figure in their lives that they choose him. My son was now a teenager, and I was aware he needed a father to look up to and to do men's things with, and as well having two children of a similar age to mine, this man didn't drink or smoke, and he often gave good advice to the children. So, my ears pricked up when I heard my children say that they would like him to be their dad.

This was ten years on from the divorce with the father of my children, and I had not been dating in that time because I was working hard to establish security for myself and the children. I now had a three-bedroom town house, beautifully decorated and furnished, with no debt. I also drove a top-of-the-range BMW, fully paid for, and feeling like a real high-flyer, I was certainly not looking to bring a man into my life. However, my children were my weakness, and so he used his hidden manipulation skills to get them to persuade me to marry him. They thought he was the perfect father figure, just what we needed to make our family complete, but whilst it might have worked well for them, him and his two children, what about me?

I had started digging the pit

I realised my mistake on my wedding night, as we made love for the first time and I was left feeling empty. There was no connection, he didn't even kiss me. No passion was shown, and no real intimacy was felt. I had made a big mistake, but I told myself that it would get better as long as my children had the father figure they so badly needed. Plus, I had gained two lovely adopted children that needed a mother, so I embraced them as my very own.

Unfortunately, I had walked into a trap of my own making, creating a family for the right motives, but without seriously thinking it all through. I knew I didn't love him, and that it would only ever be a marriage of convenience, as he was a good father to my children, and I a good mother to his. I think of them as my own to this day. None of that changes the fact that I had started digging the pit, which was going to prove costly down the road.

Over the next six years, his true misogynistic personality came through, seizing control of my life and eventually costing me my home and the business we had built up together, testing my resilience and self-worth to the maximum. I had given him free rein over my life without him giving any consideration to my needs, desires or hopes, and I often felt like the third wheel as his obsessive attention was so much on my daughter instead of me.

This continued for years as it was all about our children's needs, and I was just the third party, working to pay for all their educational needs, as he would use all our business money to do his private business on his side line. I was doing my part of the arrangement, but was he?

My Lifelines

- Never allow anybody to use you to gain their goals and not reward you. That is not what you signed up for.

- Don't let your children's needs overshadow your own.

- Teach your children about the balance of a father, mother and child relationship.

- If you only like a part of him, and catch a flicker of warning signs (think frog in the boiling pot), address it straight away or run.

- If a man does not kiss you spontaneously and with passion whilst courting, run. The rest will only be mechanical, without heart or soul.

- A marriage is between man and a woman, not a man and the children.

- If in doubt, listen to that little voice – 'Don't do it!'

- Don't ever marry for money or, as in my case, for the children's sake. It never works, as you will never be satisfied.

- Marry because you like him. He should be your best friend, and he needs to have the same values and background (and preferably faith), with no substance abuse. Then, if you also believe he will be a good father, allow the sexual magic and love to flow.

- Not all storms come to disrupt your life. Some are here to clear your path.

CHAPTER 12

The Shadows of My Childhood

It's not the depth of the wound that counts, but the size of the scar it leaves on your heart and soul, as that is what can dictate your life's choices.

In the heart of Africa, in what was then called Northern Rhodesia (now Zambia), my average Dutch Family emigrated to the 'Copperbelt,' where the smell of tobacco fields and barns scented the rich atmosphere of our exciting new life on my Uncle Cliff's farm, where all the houses had thatched roofs and red-polished cement floors.

There is a charm to Africa that still has me yearning to go back to the rawness of it all. I remember being a carefree three-year-old with one goal for the day: to play outside, doing the things like making mud pies, which were really more like clay pies, as the sand we played in was silky, fine and reddish-brown, and solidified very quickly when water was added. This is where the original clay pots came from and our playground with the local children, where we sat on our haunches, eating with our hands from the black iron pot, making happy memories filled with smells and sounds of food cooking and fire burning.

I was a free-spirited, happy little girl, not needing much attention as the curiosity of the outdoors and my new local friends were enough. Besides, being the youngest of five girls, my mother had her hands full navigating the new language of English that my sisters' homework was demanding, so I was left to my own devices quite a bit.

One of the highlights of my childhood days was riding in the Bedford pickup truck with my Uncle Cliff as he did his rounds of the farm, and he seemed to enjoy all the 'why?' questions of a little chatterbox child sitting on the seat next to him. In and out of the pickup, I was like his little shadow as he went about his daily stops, but one day I didn't realise that I had not closed the door properly. It needed to be slammed in order to lock, and we were driving on the remote, sandy farm road, navigating the high built-up areas where stumps of grass hid the rocks, when the front right-hand wheel struck a rock. As the left door was ajar, my slight three-year-old body bounced and rolled out, landing under the back left hand wheel just in time for it to roll right over my pelvis. I don't remember anything else except the shaking as he ran miles with my limp little body in his arms, panting and shouting for help from the workers in their native language.

My next memory is of lying on the couch, hearing my mother's soothing voice as she stroked my head softly, whilst I slipped in and out of consciousness.

My life changed that day, thanks to the impact and ripple effect that the accident had, and my sweet Uncle Cliff never managed to forgive himself for what happened. I remember him being very distracted and sad when, in my childhood way of asking why I couldn't go with him in the truck anymore, I asked him why he was grumpy. His life had changed, too, and I only wish I had the opportunity now, as an adult, to help him through the self-forgiveness process that I now know and have practised myself.

For the following years to come, I was always being carried on my father's shoulders or sitting on his lap, or in a wheelbarrow being pushed around by my sisters and friends.

Knowing the truth will set you free

During that time of dependency in my early years, I was bathed and taken to the toilet mostly by my father, as I had cast after cast put around my thorax that kept my legs apart in a frog-like position (my family and friends called me Froggy, in an attempt to lighten the awkwardness of it). Things happened that should not have, and the extent of that was so deep that it took me until age fifty-five to find a truth buried so deep in my subconscious mind, I needed some serious mentoring to bring it to the surface.

I had always known that my relationship with my father was different than what he had with my sisters, and when the truth of it came out, the shock and relief were palpable as things finally started making sense and falling into place.

My father had molested me in that period, though how much and for how long, I would never know. I was helpless and could not move the lower part of my body, and the experience must have been so traumatic that I blocked it out of my mind and unwittingly manifested its impact through my choice of partners.

> *The betrayed trust and misuse of authority had such a profound effect on me that I ended up going through life never trusting men and always wanting them to protect me.*

Sharing the truth with my mother freed her, as she had always suspected something was off, but was too busy and could not articulate her uneasy feelings. She was always downplaying or being harsher with me, even just indirectly, but after this revelation, my relationship with her became deep and very special, bringing us very close in her final years.

My freedom had been taken away, as not only was I dependent and restricted in my little body, I was also restricted in my need to discover new things, as any child needs.

I realise that I am still that little girl now, hating to be restricted or tied down, and only wanting to be *me*, whoever I was in my life. Hence the continual journey of finding my truth; my unique identity.

My journey through abuse was underway

> *Being free to choose to forgive is the most*
> *powerful experience I can think of in my life.*

It is why still today I am always seeking the truth in any situation, mostly in human behaviour, with my two highest values being RESPECT and TRUTH. Respect meaning self-respect, as we all have a past or a shadow that hasn't been exposed yet, but we are free to choose to bring those shadows forth and prevent them from silently dictating our lives.

There's nothing new under the sun. You are not the only person who has been exposed to this, whatever 'this' happens to be. I guarantee you, others have been exposed to the same thing.

> *It's not the depth of the wound that counts, but*
> *the size of the scar it leaves on your heart and soul,*
> *as that is what dictates your life's choices.*

My shadows had defined me, but it's my choice to let them go and move forward to Live, Love and Laugh again.

My Lifelines

- By knowing my truth, I am stronger.

- I am smarter because my truth is exposed.

- I am happier because I have overcome my pain.

- Now I know I am wiser, as I have learned from my own pain.

- Don't dwell on what happened, but think about how to heal and cancel it.

- Don't overthink, as you will cause the problem to expand and grow.

- Never force the unknown, as you will find a problem that wasn't there in the first place.

- Always seek professional guidance when the past shows up.

- If you find you are depressed, you are living in Your Past.

- If you are anxious, you are living in Your Future.

- If you are living in peace, you are living in Your Now.

CHAPTER 13

The Potholes of Life

'Mom, you are like a child hopping and skipping in a landmine field, never touching one to set it off.'

Have you ever said the 'oops!' word or had an 'OMG (Oh my gosh), what did I get myself into?' moment? During my lifetime, I have several times managed to get myself into situations that I later realised I could and should have avoided.

Was the issue that I cannot say no, or is it just that I was interested in new things, acquaintances and challenges? My Children (now as adults) always say that they keep getting surprised at how I get myself in and out of situations that I ignorantly or innocently find myself in. My son says, 'Mom, you are like a child hopping and skipping in a landmine field, never touching one to set it off', and that was true.

This made me think back on my life through his eyes, and it gave me a reality check. Was I ignorant, innocent or both? Or just adventurous, which comes with the territory?

One such situation that came to mind was when my female doctor friend and I travelled by car from Botswana to Tanzania. Yes, two women in an old Ford Station Wagon, off to work in a small African Village for two weeks. Our enthusiasm and passion to get to the village with the medical supplies and treatment was a big motivation to get there as soon as possible, and, typical of us woman, we did all the preparation ourselves beforehand, making sure the supplies were packed and the doses were calculated to the finest detail. However, I never checked, or even thought about, tools in case we got a flat tire, which for a three-day road trip on African roads was crazily irresponsible.

Fuelled with enthusiasm and anticipation

Off Wendy and I went, leaving home in the early hours as the sun was just rising on the horizon. Stocked with plenty of snacks and water, fuelled by enthusiasm and hopeful anticipation, and only stopping on the roadside having a break before the sun became too hot to stop.

Driving through the different landscapes, we were aware that we were traveling in the more primitive, vast areas that were beautiful in their sacristy of trees and absence of life, except for the signage warning to beware of wild animals crossing the road. We cruised along at a steady pace until we started to swerve between the potholes in the road, which were scarcely spread, with some over 80cm deep and half a meter wide, capable of seriously damaging our wheels. It thus became a massively stressful drive, and virtually impossible to get to our next destination before dark.

You cannot drive fast and skip over them; you cannot drive slowly, as you will get stuck in them. Avoiding them was impossible, a hopeless situation with no way out but through. It was a real 'up to you' moment. Potholes in the road, as in life, come in all shapes, sizes and depths.

Some come with warning signs, though mostly unseen until you are forced to react, stop, swerve or find another way round.

A reality of life is that we reach points where we cannot avoid potholes. It could be the inevitability of divorce, continual abuse or your child's substance abuse issues. All these circumstances have to be faced head on, like a pothole in the road. You know you cannot ignore it or avoid it, and just have to go through it head-on.

The opportunity to face your potholes will impact all that follows. Your only option is acceptance, which may take as long as it takes in your unique circumstances. Only then can you find the remedy and answers to a way forward.

The sooner you can come to terms with the whole situation, the sooner the answers will come

There are so many 'what ifs' or 'could haves' moments in life, causing much inner conflict when facing these potholes. What could I have done differently? Could I have seen the potholes? What could I have done to prevent myself hitting this precarious stretch of my journey?

This could be the guilt that is stopping you from accepting the reality of the potholes, and it will eat you from the inside out if you let it. The feelings of helplessness and hopelessness paralyse every action, and the potholes get deeper and more profound. Just like driving through the potholes damages the car and can bring it to a standstill, the figurative potholes damage and affect your whole life.

Finding yourself on this potholed road in day-to-day life can be mitigated by the support of trusted family and friends or professional support, acting like a spare wheel or a breakdown company.

Facing the truth head-on, asking the following questions:

- What can I do positively right now, for them or the situation, and myself?
- Who can I trust to support me, having possibly gone through similar circumstances themselves?
- How can I possibly get clarity for me to know what, where and how?
- What is my motivation, and what are the possible outcomes and emotional impacts for myself and my family?
- What time frames are realistically available, and what is most important to be addressed first?

Feeling it, being it and then letting it go!

So, some of the answers that became a reality of becoming aware of my actual feelings and being truthful, by realising that shock, anger, disgust, loss, hopelessness, lack of direction and feeling stuck and sad, and just not coping, can be embraced.

In my own situations, I arrived at the stage where I did not allow myself to express outwardly these powerful emotions, and by burying them deep within me, I made myself ill, which manifested in the years that followed each trauma and test. This included vertigo, IBS, depression and allergies.

As much as I thought I was looking for the truth, I actually looked for the truth in the situation, rather than the truth that was controlling my everyday life. Know the truth, and the truth will set you free and allow the healing to start. This is your 'bounce back muscle,' which you have to fire up in order to condition yourself to listen to your feelings and emotions, and to embrace them in the moment.

Feeling it, being it and letting it go!

You are not your emotions. You merely experience them

Through these experiences, I learned to step aside and allow myself to look deeply into myself with honesty and without self-criticism, allowing all the emotions and feelings to come to the surface, even if it meant screaming, kicking, hitting a pillow and sobbing my heart out. I always felt relieved afterwards, and was able to face the next day's challenges.

We are flesh and blood, not stone. We are complex in all forms and extremely fragile, but not broken; just experiencing a moment that will pass.

Just like these pebbles, we are shaped by the storms and the continuous movement of the currents we find ourselves in.

You can stand out as an individual and be who *you* uniquely are, and make an impact on all those around you, or you can choose to blend in and fade into the background, with all your suffering and the lessons learned having no purpose or value to others in need.

My view is that my own traumas, pain and tears were actually worth it if the result is that other women and men feel they now have hope and become empowered to live, love and laugh again.

My Lifelines

- Look in the mirror, what do you see? Allow yourself to be you.

- I suddenly knew it was time to start a new me, and that through the power of trusting the process, I would get the right answers.

- Just because things are not happening for me right now, it doesn't mean they will never happen.

- I know if I keep doing the same thing, I will keep getting the same results.

- I actively embrace my daily change.

- Change is imminent, so don't stop it.

- You have two choices: to go against it or to embrace it.

- In any given moment, we have two options: stepping forward into growth or stepping backwards into safety.

- Expectation and wanting the answers is a transformation of its own.

- I became the force of change because I was teachable and willing to grow.

- Being happy the way I am, but prepared to change for the better, is what gives me the power to rise above any situation and transform into a stronger, better version of myself.

- I believe it, and that settles it.

JOKÉ HOETMER

CHAPTER 14

I'm Not a Super Woman or Super Mom!

The Reality of Grief When it Strikes

Grief comes in many forms and is individual to each of us. As I know to my own cost there is no prescriptive answer, we have to face up to the truth and deal with it as best we can. Its a rainy, cold winter morning and whilst stretching my body, I try to open my eyes. They feel as if I have sand in them, as I had rubbed them so much throughout the night. Squinting through the slits, I notice my hair. It looks as if I have a bird's nest on my head. Sighing with my shoulders bent over, I shuffle back into the comfort of the warm bed and pull the duvet over my head. Sleep, just sleep is all I need...

This went on for days, as I did the bare minimum, very unlike me.

For the first time, I had allowed myself to embrace all the stages of grief. Being just after a family death, so in operation mode to help the family and make all the necessary arrangements, I had not allowed myself to feel the pain before now. It was like a water bubble bursting, and I could no longer contain it.

Throughout this process, I was quite shocked at myself and the true feelings that came out. Yes, I knew all about the different stages of mourning, being a trained nurse, but there was another angle that I was ashamed of, the cherry on top of the pain of having previously lost two sons, a son-in-law and my stepson, who I was awfully close to, at the age of just twenty-one. Again, I made sure all the family and my children were cared for, and that all the practical things were organised, but *I never allowed myself to grieve*. I never had the tears or all the emotions that I needed to face.

Now, however, the dam had burst and I could not stop it. During this process, to my shame, I became angry with God. My mind knew that it was not the way to go, but my heart and emotions would not let up. I was angry with God because how, when I did all the right things, had they still died? Why would a merciful God let this happen? The feelings just got worse, and the tears started drying up. I decided I had had enough of God.

This is a typical example of the black dog and white dog fighting. Which dog will win? The one you feed, of course. I knew this, but could not get out of that space of anger, even though it was not as strong as in the previous weeks.

Alan, my son-in-law, was only thirty-two when he died. He was the best thing that could have happened to my adopted daughter. He was an excellent young dad to his two children, the youngest being just three years old, and the anger I felt as he was resuscitated four times after an asthma-induced heart attack was consuming. His wife and children saw the whole thing, as I performed the first two resuscitations whilst waiting for the ambulance to arrive. The conflict I felt as a mother and grandmother wishing to protect them from the pain was not good. They were getting along so well despite many ups and downs, and now this?

It was so sad that a little family should be broken up at such a tender time in all their lives.

This being just after I had lost Rick, my stepson, who was in and out of our family's life until, at the age of eighteen, he came back to our family as he was going to university nearby. He was such a talented young man with the world at his feet. Gifted in all academics, sports and the arts, he was, however, also a very troubled young man, as he never knew his father (the father of my children). His mother and I were remarkably close through the years, as she had more children with another husband, but Rick always felt the need to get to know his own father. I told him as much as I could, but it was obvious that he needed to speak to his mother about his feelings. Discussing the need for her to talk to him about this, we agreed to send him home.

It did not happen as planned, though. He got home, took his mother's revolver out of the safe and committed suicide. I was shattered, and never spoke to his mother again. The pain and unanswered questions about why he took this drastic step and what signs we had missed were too much. The loss was creating turmoil in my heart, and I later started blaming myself for sending him home. This stayed with me for years, as I could not get closure.

Hindsight is a wonderful science!

With a burst of tears and giving myself time to get through the mounting thoughts about what I could, should and did not do, I got a glimpse of what trauma really does to your mind (or at least to my mind). I could not see the wood from the trees, and being alone with nobody to bounce off, I became increasingly aware that I needed help and fast.

The help came because I was open to healing and finding the truth. I started in November, seven years after the three family deaths had happened, and though I had moved to London by this time, I realised I had carried the blame for Rick's death with me. I knew that it was ridiculous to think this way, but my mind just could not shake it off. I forgave myself and forgave all involved, but still could not get the mourning process going.

At the time, I was livestreaming my podcast *Raw and Real Conversations*. On the last one I did before flying back to Cape Town, I boldly said that I would contact Rick's Mom and ask her to forgive me, and after making the commitment live on social media, I spontaneously flew to sunny South Africa to spend Christmas with my children. I did not mention the subject to my daughter, and I knew she did not follow me on social media, so I was surprised when she shared that the whole of Rick's family would be staying over for Christmas.

The family arrived, and all was good as we celebrated together on Christmas Day. However, there was no opportunity to even have a moment alone with his mother. That night, I thought this through, and considered the fact that she had broken my marriage to my children's father when she became pregnant with Rick. She was only eighteen at the time, and I had forgiven her and we became friends. She was so young, and I ended up looking after the baby for her for months at a time. I loved this little boy, who was so much like my own two children, and though he went back to his mum once she got married, we remained in constant contact and he stayed close to his half-brother and sister.

At eighteen, he came back to live with us before going on to university. We all enjoyed him so much, and now, seven years after his death, I finally had the opportunity to speak to his mother in this terribly busy household and happy atmosphere. I took my chance first thing in the morning, as we both had made coffee. I said that I wanted to talk to her privately in the garden, and sitting down on the hard, cast-iron furniture, compassion came over me for this young woman who had lost her son, noting how she had aged. From that moment on, it was easy. I apologised for not supporting her in her loss, hugging her at the same time.

It was not necessary to explain what had gone through my mind about how different the outcome could have been if she had only had the open conversation with her son. I just blurted out that I was sorry it happened, and that I felt responsible for sending him, explaining that the guilt had been so strong for years. She did not respond to it at all, and yes, it sounded ridiculous, but it was real. Then, when I asked how she had coped and how she was doing, it came to mind that she was just engaging with his siblings and keeping herself busy, which made it easier not to think about it.

It was good to connect again and speak openly. Hindsight is a wonderful science, and I realised the relief I felt just by having that conversation. What a difference it made to me. I was free, even if it went right over her head what I was trying to say. I was healed, and I had needed to do that.

However, the healing of the anger I had towards God was still lurking in the back of my mind. I didn't dare to think about it, but knew it was there.

Why did I even have the audacity to think I knew better than Him? (meaning GOD himself)

My Lifeline

- It's not all up to me.

- The more pain of loss you experience is a refection of love lost.

- Embrace the pain, don't hold back as there is no format to grief.

- Expect to cry randomly, as its your expression of being true to you.

- Don't expect it to be easy, as loss comes in many waves. Just let it flow.

- Never go into the what ifs or should haves,
  as this will prolong your grief.

- Let the denial, the anger and tears flow, its healing to the soul.

- Grieve alone, grieve in public, grieve in silence,
  you are allowed to, and you are not alone.

- There is no shame in loss.

- Personal grief comes in many forms, don't try to understand it.

- Love lost always brings out the good eventually.

CHAPTER 15

This Life Is Not a Rehearsal

*Do not attract what you desire,
attract what you are*

I was asking myself, why do I keep going round the same mountain, and why don't I get off it?

I can now see how naive and fallible I was. I am not finding excuses for all the mistakes I have made, but I do need to ask myself how I got into these situations in the first place? I have had enough of it; enough of the consistent abuse and the trauma it causes, not only to me, but my children and close family.

Fantasising about what the ideal husband or relationship was going to be

In a household of six girls, in a three-bedroom, moderate house with one bathroom, it took some juggling on a school morning. Having the only toilet in the house in the one bathroom required us to think of creative ways to go to the loo. When it was Dad's turn to use the toilet, he would always be in a sitting position, and we did not know any better. Much to my dismay, later in life, I saw my sister's boyfriend standing in the garden, as there was no way he could get to the toilet indoors in time. That evening, I shared this at the dinner table, and we all had a good laugh at the lack of exposure to the opposite sex, being an all-girl household except for poor Dad, of course. We were aware how close we were as a family, and becoming teenagers, we were curious about boys.

In those days, there was no television or internet, and only single-sex schools, so the only way of meeting somebody was through school socials or church youth clubs.

The absence of boys growing up in our lives had its disadvantages. We had no idea how to interact with them, and I remember every Saturday, my teenage sister and I had to clean windows. She chose to wash outside, even though it was harder because she had to stand on the ladder between the bushes and flowerbeds, and I thought I had the better deal washing inside. However, her plan was to see and be seen by the passing boys. I remember how ridiculous she looked, and how she acted as the boys cycled by, and by the time I was sixteen, I ended up in boarding school across two borders, going from Zambia to South Africa. Here, my relationship journey began. Never quite getting the full picture, and relying on my own references of boys and men.

Fantasising about what the ideal husband or relationship was going to be, I found that I was never content and was on a quest to find bliss, always looking for more. Maybe I could have become quite promiscuous, but having a very strict upbringing and moral standing wrapped up in loyalty, I thankfully never succumbed to that way of life. Instead, to my dismay as the years passed, I kept getting married.

When trauma or abuse of some sort happens in your formative years, you may find refuge residing in a fantasy world. For me, it was a subconscious coping strategy, a survival mechanism.

Many years later, at fifty-five, finding myself divorced again, the desperate search for the truth was stirring in my soul. How could I not see the patterns I was repeating before it was too late?

Here I go, into internal overdrive to find
my deepest unknown. WHY?

Soul-searching through various sessions, I soon realised I was blinded by the busyness of my life and needed to survive financially in order to keep the boat afloat. Why did I do that? Because I could, and because it was my performance default to work hard. It's who I was − I never gave up.

I was finding the courage to start again, the strength
to endure the truth and resolve to finish

Facing the truth takes courage, and by intentionally looking for the answer, after continuously finding myself desperate to get out of the cycle of the marriage destruction and the hopelessness, I found it very helpful to be able to talk about my feelings to a counsellor or trusted friend. I wanted to see the part I played in this whole saga, so I kept asking the unanswered questions: what's wrong with me? Do I deserve this? What did I do wrong? The self-doubt hit me hard, like the battle between the white dog and the black dog.

Self-doubt was becoming very familiar. The shame of another divorce clouded my every action, along with the fear of failure and all the blame that follows. I found it hard to express my hurt and articulate the feelings that I carried. Mostly self-inflicted, my destruction was part of a downward spiral, as behavioural and thought patterns continued to weaken me.

The ending of a marriage can be gut-wrenching

Sometimes, the decision to divorce is a practical one, steeped in logic and rational thought. Often, though, it is a messy, complicated and downright emotional rollercoaster.

The end of a marriage can be gut-wrenching. Like those bad movies, we only wish we could take away all the bad and boring parts of the divorce process, and edit it all back together again to bring you right to the end. Wanting to be grounded again and to get a bit of perspective, I was alone and lonely without financial security, and had no hope for myself or my children's futures. The questions, judgements and sympathy that I was experiencing was causing me to be even harder on myself, as I tried to explain how behind closed doors things looked different than they did on the outside, referring to the arguments and resentment.

In searching for and confronting these issues, I felt as though I was reopening old wounds, and doors into my life, that I'd long since closed off. In real terms, were these my blind spots?

I had become a different person, and the day came where I had to wake up and ask myself, 'Who on earth is this stranger I'm married to, and how could I ever love him?'

I had stopped feeling, and my tears were now silent. That's when I was a danger to the relationship, as there was nothing left to hold on to.

Cheating is a very emotive subject. It does happen in the physical realm, and can be related to a whole host of pragmatic problems (eg distance or sexual incompatibility), but it also falls into the realm of emotional problems because it can fundamentally change the way you feel about your partner. Even if you are willing to give him or her another chance and work through it, the emotional damage is done. Trust issues (another practical reason for divorce with strong ties to the emotional) are now a given, and you might never be able to trust your partner again, even if you badly want to. For me, I felt disrespected, and the little bit of self-respect and value I had left was enough for me to say: 'No more!' I would not accept this betrayal of my value and the beauty of marriage.

There was also a lack of intimacy, and not just sexual, either. We never spoke anymore, never cuddled or spent alone time, as he was gradually being consumed by his work and the hobbies that took him away from home. The hopes, dreams and aspirations we once shared seem to no longer be subjects of conversation, and the lack of intimacy made it even more confusing. He seemed to find satisfaction in hurting me emotionally by withdrawing from me and only having sex once he had brought me to tears through an argument that I had no way of winning. I say 'sex' rather than 'making love' because there was no kissing or emotional bonding. It was as if I was a prostitute and he was just doing the deed, but without putting the money down on the table when he left at the end.

Resentment was to follow. This lack of respect, and my allowing it, caused me to resent the fact that I allowed it to happen every time. He was an expert in letting me take the blame, and the resentment became so real that it ruined all my feelings. The conversations just got worse when I tried to explain myself, as both of us were keeping a tally and the resentment was getting harder to shed.

Being resentful of the attention he gave my children was a major wakeup call for me. How I was able to reconcile that being the source of conflict, as who does not want their husband to give their children attention? That was not the issue, though. It was the possessive and obsessive attention that built up resentment, and I could not do anything about it. Being truthful with yourself is very painful, but it is also an absolute necessity before you can grow and change for the better. I wanted to change, and to let go of the resentment.

In addition to the heated arguments, the silent body language can be an argument in itself. It can be nice to have a peaceful environment, but it never happened as it became obvious to the children that things were very bad. A lot of arguments of this kind can be mistaken for passion, but whilst arguing is a sign that you are committed to working out the differences in your relationship (to a point), issues that never resolve themselves are not a sign of a healthy or happy relationship. Worst of all, being at war with the person who is supposed to be your pillar and partner in life can leave you emotionally drained and keep you from investing yourself into your relationship. I withdrew, albeit unintentionally, as it was just part of the emotional abuse dance.

Outside of cheating, I also started noticing compulsive lying, and sometimes found it very hard to figure out what he was trying to hide. The really bad thing was that the older children saw this and began thinking it was okay to tell half-truths and that they could get away with it. This really stressed me out, as I didn't confront him because I wanted to keep the peace in the home, and it's impossible to punish the children for lying when their father is doing that very thing, and I am not doing anything about it.

> **If you can't trust your partner to pay the bills**
> **on time and not spend the money elsewhere,**
> **what have you actually got to hold on to?**

If you know your partner will make promises they'll never follow up on, you have a fundamental problem of trust in your relationship; one that affects you emotionally.

> **The men who love strong woman and set out to destroy**
> **them – the profile of a MISOGYNIST. The help I needed**
> **to know, as I felt I had lost my mind with all his antics.**

It's not only distrust at play here, but also the false pretence that leads to false hope that maybe your partner will change this time, and the inevitable disappointment that happens nine times out of ten when they don't.

Jealousy and insecurity can see a form of trust issues, but they are really their own thing. I found that even though I am in no way, shape or form a jealous person, deep in my heart I was jealous of all the attention my husband was giving everyone else but me. I found myself doubting my very existence and value. I was not wanting a relationship to be all about my husband spending every moment of every day with me (in actual fact, I gave him all the freedom he wanted, never checking on him or doubting his actions, and I didn't think for one minute I needed him reassuring me), but he only ever did just enough to keep me at bay. That was how it was for years, till I started reading the book *Men Who Hate Women, the Women Who Love Him* by Susan Forward, which gave me the answers to understanding what I was dealing with.

I was constantly questioning why, breaking down my self-esteem and making me feel very inferior, even though I knew I was anything but. This man, my second husband, showed all the traits of a misogynist. 'He was a man who disliked, despised and was strongly prejudiced against me,' or perhaps, 'He was always a man who hated women emotionally stronger than him, who could be a male chauvinist, who thinks all women are stupid and manipulative.'

Typical Traits of a Misogynist, according to Berit Brogaard DMSci, PhD

1. He will zero in on a woman and choose her as his target. Her natural defences may be down because he's flirtatious, exciting, fun, and charismatic at first.
2. As time goes on, he begins to reveal a Jekyll & Hyde personality. He may change quickly from irresistible to rude, and from rude back to irresistible.

3. He will make promises to women and often fail to keep them. With men, on the other hand, he will almost always keep his word.
4. He will be late for appointments and dates with women but be quite punctual with men.
5. His behaviour toward women in general is grandiose, cocky, controlling, and self-centred.
6. He is extremely competitive, especially with women. If a woman does better than him socially or professionally, he feels terrible. If a man does better, he may have mixed feelings about it, but he is able to look at the situation objectively.
7. He will unknowingly treat women differently from men in the workplace and social settings, allowing men various liberties for which he will criticize female colleagues or friends.
8. He will be prepared (unconsciously) to use anything within his power to make women feel miserable. He may demand sex or withhold sex in his relationships, make jokes about women or put them down in public, "borrow" their ideas in professional contexts without giving them credit, or borrow money from them without paying them back.
9. On a date, he will treat a woman the opposite of how she prefers. If she is an old-style lady who prefers a "gentleman" who holds the door for her, orders for both and pays for the meal, he will treat her like one of his male buddies, order for himself, and let her pay for the whole meal if she offers (and sometimes even if she doesn't). If she is a more independent type who prefers to order her own meal and pay for herself, he will rudely order for both and pay the check while she goes to the bathroom.
10. Sexually, he likes to control women and gives little or no attention to their sexual pleasure. Foreplay, if it occurs at all, is only a necessary means to an end. He likes oral sex but only as a recipient. His favourite positions enable him to avoid looking the woman in her eyes.
11. He will cheat on women he is dating or in a relationship with. Monogamy is the last thing he feels he owes a woman.

12. He may suddenly disappear from a relationship without ending it, but may come back three months later with an explanation designed to lure the woman back in.

Only rarely will a misogynist possess every one of these traits, which makes it harder to identify them. Their ability to lure women in with their charm and charisma adds to the difficulty of spotting the early-warning signs.

Women haters (unconsciously) get off on treating women badly. Every time they can put down a woman or hurt her feelings, they unconsciously feel good because deep down in their hidden brain, their bad behaviour is rewarded with a dose of the pleasure chemical dopamine—which makes them want to repeat the behaviour again and again.

JOKÉ HOETMER

CHAPTER 16

Chaos in Your Crisis

Fight one more round

My journey of self-discovery and finding the true meaning of love and life's purpose has seen me experience the loss of a successful business through no fault of my own, which also involved total betrayal by my husband and business partner, who left with both the money and my best friend. This journey, as I have previously mentioned in other chapters, has also forced on me to suffer physical and emotional abuse, before slowly but surely rebuilding a new life for myself and my children.

Just like so many other women across the world whose love journey has taken so many twists and turns, with their own tears behind the smiles, suffering trauma, rejection, and betrayal, feelings of conflict, shame and constant self-doubt looming in my subconscious mind.

Pity Parties were Never Allowed

I could give way to these feelings of hopelessness and sink into pity parties, or I could do what I did and choose to embrace the pain, the lessons and the journey with a drive to always try to do the right thing. This caused me to go through these lessons that are varied and dramatic, and so real to life in so many ways, for so many women living through similar circumstances today.

Putting resilience into overdrive

I was sitting in a boardroom with twelve upright, uncomfortable chairs and a table far too big for the room. The dim lighting flickered lightly, and I felt intimidated by the atmosphere as I sat opposite the solicitor and buyers, the latter being two Indian accountants who wanted to purchase our family business, all looking more like undertakers in their black suits with stern faces, shuffling through their mountains of paper work.

Being very aware that I was totally out of my depth here, I felt the tension rising as I waited, feeling this intense loneliness and apprehension, with only my little black briefcase on my lap, smiling nervously whilst trying to compose myself. It was all very surreal, with my husband and business partner's absence very conspicuous, leaving me to singlehandedly represent my side of the sale.

The business in question was industrial catering equipment. The stakes were high, as we were discussing a lot of money, and as the negotiations started, there was sudden prompting in my spirit, stirring up the boldness to challenge them head-on regarding specific points of the contract. Their shocked reaction caused a shift in the atmosphere and a muttering between themselves, which resulted in the solicitor excusing himself from the room in order to rectify (yes, rectify!) the contract to my liking.

Hardly believing what was happening, and now feeling much less intimidated and more in control for a brief moment, the deal was almost done, with only the formality of signing the contract remaining. The feeling of accomplishment swept over me as I sat up, ready to sign the paperwork.

Then, I was told that I didn't have to sign anything... What, why not?

Like a punch in the stomach, the news hit me, almost causing me to fall off my chair in shock, as they informed me that only my husband had signing power, since he was the sole owner of the company. I was blinded and betrayed big time!

He had gone behind my back and changed ownership of the company without my knowledge, tricking me into putting the deal together, doing the negotiating and stressing all the while, working and believing that I was an equal partner in the business. It quickly dawned on me that I would never get the share of the money I was expecting for all the hard work and sacrifice, as my husband has just sold our business and gone on a safari with my share of the money.

Driving back to my family home, trying to unpick the reality what was happening, my mind was spinning with shock and disbelief. I called a family friend, Brian, to share what was happening, and how my world was collapsing around me.

Brian is such a gentle giant, always filled with love and a kind, encouraging word, so I knew he would cheer me up and give me sound advice.

Little did I know, matters were going to take an ever crazier and worse direction than they had already.

'Brian, I am leaving Botswana and going to live with my children in South Africa,' I blurted out.

There was a long silence, and then he gave some more devastating news into my life, sounding vastly different from the usual strong voice I was used to.

'He is with my wife'

'Brian, what's wrong?' I asked, concerned, but barely hearing him through his tears.

'Joké, do you know where your husband is?'

'Yes, he is on a safari doing his thing' I answered quickly with no thought behind it.

'No, Joké, he isn't,' he said, before pausing to take a deep breath. 'He is with my wife. He has been with her for the last five weeks. It's been going on for over a year.'

You could hear a pin drop. Time stood still. No words would come, as the rollercoaster of mixed emotions set off, could this really be happening to me? Was this for real?

Still reeling from the realisation that the business had gone from under me, I couldn't take it all in. So many unanswered questions were making my head spin. The betrayal. The lies. How did I not see this? The man I loved and trusted was having an affair with our best friend right under my nose, and her husband, our close friend, Brian is broken on the other end of this phone call.

In one morning, my world completely fell apart. Suddenly, nothing was the same, as what started off as an exciting business deal turned into my biggest nightmare.

Be Willing to Rest in your Incubator, to Grow and Become an Innovator

'I know I want a house with five bedrooms, close to the schools. A loft room and a view would be a bonus,' I say confidently, as I am driving with the estate agent to view a property in sunny South Africa. I was desperately trying to relocate and find a home for us, away from him in Botswana.

She smiles and I smile back, hoping that she does not become aware that I don't have the money.

'I'd love to have a repossessed house that's a fixer upper,' I add, launching into a conversation about my love for renovating homes.

Within a few days, she finds the one and I sign the letter of intent to purchase, knowing that I really need to play for time; time to find the money somehow. That same evening, I go back to the house to take down the *For Sale* board, mentally proclaiming that the house is mine already. I give the security guard instructions to clean up the garden and buy him cigarettes and a Coke, which seems to get him going.

This house is sold, it's mine. Now, I just need to pay for it.

With my survival instinct piqued and my inner resilience in overdrive, I start working on a plan to create the future my children and I deserve. One by one, every step in the plan falls into place. I take bold steps towards the purchase of the house; the agent calls with the good news that my offer has been accepted, and is taken aback by my lack of surprise. **I trusted and took action.** My courier is already on the way to that address with our furniture from Botswana, I explain. She is shocked and surprised by my faith or stupidity, I guess.

Over the next few days, I get resourceful with the property deals I shared with my now estranged husband. I take careful stock of what is on hand and what is available to explore and monetise. The innovation of finding cashflow just followed, as I did most of the deals in the first place. So now the deposit was paid, followed by the transfer fees and, again, I carefully consider my resources, my resourcefulness, my negotiation skills and my experience and pure desperation fuelled by determination, and I did it!

Each of us has an arsenal of skills and experiences we can draw from if we stop panicking and carefully consider what they are. As more plans fall into place, my confidence grows and my steps get bolder. My faith and trust swell, and as a result, I accomplish more.

Using an advance from the bank, I commission the building of a flat with a garage next to the house, which I quickly rent out. The rental income pays for the bond in total whilst my children and I live in the house. I still smile when I think of all the wonderful memories we shared in that home over the years. We lived in the house through their schooling, university, marriages and even my very first grandchild. I realise things could have looked quite different had I not reached deep into my inner resolve, strength and resilience during one of the biggest tests of my lifetime.

My Lifelines

- I've learned to make peace with myself through self-
  forgiveness and the removal of blame and shame,
  which is, by the way, the hardest thing to do.

- Believing in the forgiveness of others, directly or indirectly.

- Finding contentment when I am uncomfortable or feel out of control.

- Coming to terms with the situation as quickly as possible by allowing
  myself to feel the pain, loss or fear; deciding to let it go and move on.

- Finding the courage and determination to get out of
  bed in the morning, wash my face and to say to myself,
  'I can do this. Today is going to be a good day.'

- Finding somebody to be accountable to and taking baby steps
  towards recovery, through constantly encouraging myself
  and humouring myself (laughter is the best medicine). I find
  my children and grandchildren really help in that regard.

- Reach out to others who you respect for advice and
  allow yourself to be teachable in every possible facet
  of your life. This helps you to see more clearly.

- Never compare yourself to others and their journey, but rather
  respect those you admire and be inspired to learn from them.

- Only follow people that inspire you and allow
  them to push your personal boundaries.

- Getting quiet is the SOS in life.

- Show up to love yourself and choose to live.

- Stay true to yourself.

- Never be afraid to fall, to fail and to get back up again.

Business is there to be made. Just find the spot and walk towards it

Every obstacle, every disaster, every failed business transaction since that day, I've met with the same resilience and resolve. It is always there for us to access and drink from. It is a fountain that never stops flowing.

In fact, it flows stronger and stronger the more we drink from it.

'Bounce back muscle'

I have heard many people refer to resilience as a 'bounce back muscle.' The more adversity we face and overcome, the quicker and faster our bounce back is, and the higher we bounce when we get back up. Something like a ball that is forced under the water in a swimming pool, and with all the body weight you can muster, it will force itself out of the water and bounce right out of the water, even higher than the surface, as it bounces back. Be that ball and bounce right back to being even better and stronger than before.

As Winston Churchill famously said: 'Never, never, never give up.'

> **'Start by doing what's necessary, then do what's possible, and suddenly you are doing the impossible.' – *Francis of Assisi***

CHAPTER 17

Choose Your Battles

I became a Conqueror, not Conquered. A victor, not a victim. An Overcomer, not overcome by my situation. I chose and won my battles, so can you!

'There are three people in my marriage,' Princess Diana said, in her interview with Martin Bashir.

Yes, I said to myself, *that's where I am.*

After the major success of leaving my second husband, yes embarrassing to say I found myself in another marriage of a different kind. Judge me if you like, as I sure judged myself! Obviously I still had lessons to learn. This one so very different than those previously... How many times did I feel the knowing that I was not allowing the real truth to be faced. The elephant in the room that I never dared address for fear of rattling the cage and letting it loose.

The Elephant in the Room

When you have a second marriage, or even a third, you always have the baggage of previous wives or children to consider, especially if you have a blended family. I had managed the blending beautifully in the past, as our children were of similar ages and got on well.

Bonding the children was like running a business to me. Each child had his or her special place and talents and personality to bring to the table. The business (family) ethos was to RESPECT one another, and to always have a voice that was heard. I would not allow the children to tattle-tale or badmouth one another, and encouraged them to learn to express themselves and embrace their differences. It worked, as we had family meetings every Sunday where anything could be discussed; grievances and ideas were shared as we planned the next week. This included us parents as well. We were all equal around the table, as we resolved lots of differences as a result of mutual respect and understanding, creating a well-adjusted family unit (see Chapter 7).

Being a victim of my own moral standing and trying to do the right thing

This was different, though. My husband was poorly at the time I married him, having just had open heart surgery. He was broken and broke following a very bad divorce, so not exactly a good catch, however we married as the circumstances were rushed in many ways. The week before we got married, I still had doubts, but everything was now in motion and I didn't want to let others down. I reminded myself that he was a good man, and I knew his family and they had a good history (this is what caused me to lower my defences), and I figured that if he was anything like them, it would all be good.

Once again, hindsight is a wonderful science.

On our wedding night, my husband chose to sleep in his son's bed, the child being overwhelmed by his father getting married. I embraced the situation, thinking this was a one-off, and I never mentioned my disappointment at being left on my own the whole time on our honeymoon night. I thought this totally strange behaviour was so confusing, as we had not had a physical relationship before the marriage night. I had walked into a marriage where my husband's son was his top priority.

Being the victim of my own moral standing, and always trying to do the right thing, I embraced the boy as my own and tried to work around the imbalanced way my husband was treating him. Making his son the adult became his first priority in all aspects in the home, even confiding, and decision making that should not be on a child's shoulders, but on the parents as a unit. This was all wrong according to my boundaries and the way I was wired, triggering a loneliness that was hidden in my mind, which only grew when he came to live with us as a budding teenager.

The inner conflict this situation caused me was not healthy, but the more I tried to address it, the worse it got, to the point where I was just bobbing around trying to keep the peace in my own home, not even suggesting any alternative as my husband continued to spoil his son, making me even more introverted as I became the third person in my marriage.

At the age of sixteen, my stepson became my husband's number one, be all and end all, due to his guilt at not previously being in his life and wanting to make up for it. This led to him putting an adolescent into situations far beyond his emotional maturity, causing him to become arrogant and even controlling of his father's moods and behaviour, usually for the worse. This very unhealthy situation totally dominated the family dynamic, as my stepson fell into drinking and drug use at age seventeen, and not surprisingly followed his father's example of utilising manipulation and mind games to get whatever he wanted.

I was totally isolated from decisions made in our family business, as money was syphered off to support my stepson's hobby of quadbike racing. Only the best was good enough for him, and soon an undercurrent of frustration and anger was building up slowly, waiting to release the tension that was so embedded, and now being engraved, in my soul.

The truth is that this marriage was over long before it even began. I had actually been able to see the hand I was being dealt before the wedding, but I had no idea of the losses I would incur. This not only included losing my status as a partner in the business and wife in the relationship, but also my voice as I once again fought against myself to keep the peace.

Eventually, manipulation became threats of potential violence, not only from my husband, but also his son. They started ganging up on me, to the point where I had to learn to choose my battles between the two of them. I used the moments of clarity and connection I had with either of them to suggest the practical choices they had, or to advise something that could possibly be the answer. This worked well as long

I chose my words carefully and never gave them the chance to use anything against me, as they were like a pack of wolves, with me cast as the runt of the outfit.

My husband then started losing his grip on our business, as his source of economic stability, international fruit export, was changing. Meanwhile, his drinking and use of prescribed drugs were wearing him down. Where in the past his son was always his emotional support, he now became the burden and problem to his father. It was a love-hate situation that was painful for me to watch. I tried patching things up between them during the moments of sanity, being careful to never step on either's toes.

It was a situation that could not possibly be maintained or tolerated. I had entered into a loveless marriage, and learned when to bite my tongue and when to step up. Sadly, one example of the latter came when I was forced to go court to get a protection order, as the abuse was only escalating.

Now choosing my battles with a legal document in place, or so I thought

The court application for a restraining order was in process, but as I sat in one of the hard, straight-backed chairs provided for the defendant and the applicant, I barely noticed there were three seats in total. Then, to my surprise, in came my husband (at that time estranged) with his son in tow. As if it was not hard enough at home, I now had two against one in court, too. Still, I was hopeful that the restraining order would protect me.

Glancing at them, I couldn't help but notice how well they both looked, with my husband having had a fresh haircut and shave, looking quite handsome in his Armani jacket. Bear in mind, he had for the past three years had greasy, unkempt hair that he could tie in ponytail, and him not shaving for days on end had become the norm.

The magistrate entered the room, nodded and the formality of the questions started, asking why I wanted a restraining order as written in the application before requesting formal confirmation that I wanted to proceed.

I confidently answered yes, as it was a legal statement and everything I had said was true. I wanted to proceed, believing the law would protect me, and with great anticipation, I was ready to release a sigh of relief.

'Let's get on with this,' the magistrate said, expressionless, before inviting my estranged husband to state his case.

The system I trusted had failed me

Eloquently, my husband agreed that things had not been good in the previous three years as the business had gone under, citing the economics of the times, etc. I couldn't help but notice how the magistrate was nodding his head in agreement, as it became obvious to me that my husband was setting himself up to be the victim of circumstances, even admitting that he had been in a bad place and suffering with depression, all the while receiving nods of understanding from the magistrate. He acknowledged that he drank a bit too much, with a little, ever so charming laugh, getting the magistrate to nod again. He never mentioned his prescription drug dependency, though, which made him violent, and before the magistrate could ask any further questions, he said that his son would testify to the hardship felt at the loss of income, particularly relating to his hobby of quadbike racing.

Hang on, I thought. *Is he throwing out points of interest in order to build a rapport?*

Horrified, I saw the game he was playing. The manipulation and mind games were laid bare right in front of me, and the magistrate looked as though he was in on it, too!

Looking down at his notes, the magistrate realised he had more questions to get through. He asked if the son had anything to add, and there it all fell apart for my case and the tables turned. Here, he simply lied and said I was an abusive stepmother and that I had hit him, which caused a lot of conflict in his young life. He even looked as though he might cry at one point; acting out the victims body language that he so clearly learnt from his father.

Listening to the lies and the emphasis on the wrong places, I sunk deep into the hard, upright chair. I felt hopeless, betrayed by a boy I had loved and treated like my own, hoping that his good upbringing from his mom and me would somehow kick in eventually.

I was not prepared to get into a boxing ring
with boxers when I am not a boxer!

However prepared I was, I didn't stand a chance as the whole scene unfolded. The court order was denied, and they both walked out wearing satisfied grins as my heart sunk in utter despair at the confirmation that I had lost my voice again. Victory to them was nothing more than winning at a game, whereas for me, defeat put me in a place where my back was against the wall. I realised I could not fight this battle with a realistic chance of winning, as the system I trusted had failed me.

Walking back to the car park feeling numbed by the wrongness of it all, I was not able to find my car. My mind was a blur as I wandered about aimlessly until, exasperated, I went to get a coffee and tried to gather myself. That's when it came to me where the car was parked, outside the bakery (seeing the cakes in the coffee shop reminded me of the spot), and when I got back to it, I saw to my horror that it had been clamped.

When troubles comes knocking at the door, how many seem to appear at the same time?

It was the final straw

No way was I in a fit state to go through the release procedure at the Traffic Department. I was rattled to my core, devastated by the sheer unfairness of it all and how the system seemed set up against me. I sat down on the curb and phoned my son in-law. This was not a typical response, as usually I would call my children first, but somehow, my self-respect had gone out the window such that I went straight to the person who I knew would have a clear head in a time of crisis.

He came and immediately took charge, only asking me relevant questions as he sorted everything out and got somebody else to drive my car whilst he took me home.

My very basic need to be protected had kicked in, and I knew I wouldn't get it from my husband or the legal system. I was broken – again! – this time into even smaller pieces, as my trust in authority completely evaporated for good.

My Lifelines

- When you're losing a fight to keep somebody, it doesn't make sense to keep fighting for both of you. You know in your heart you are not a quitter. You just know when enough is enough.

- Don't keep fighting a battle that is already lost. It drains energy and finances.

- When you have given everything you have, and you are still not appreciated and still made to feel useless, for your own sanity and wellbeing, walk away.

- It can only go up from here. All I needed in this situation was to stop fighting a lost cause and move on.

- In reality, I had nothing to lose, but everything to gain by getting ME back.

- If I have nothing to struggle against, I have nothing to struggle for, apart from my value and self-respect.

- When I threw in the towel and stepped out of the boxing ring, there were two ways I could go: give up completely, or take up karate and move on.

- I lost my fear, a powerful weapon that crippled me no more.

- I had to choose to get up and fight my way back.

- Embracing the change by daily celebration of the small steps I had taken was my only hope.

JOKÉ HOETMER

CHAPTER 18

Stepping Into My Purpose Boots

Be happy with what you have, whilst working for what you want, and the courage to start, the strength to endure and the resolve to finish.

I was successful in the old brick-and-mortar business world, but this new online landscape did my head in. I wasn't feeling like I could ever master it, making me feel insignificant, miserable and overwhelmed.

There was so much more that I needed to discover, but I'd have to dig deeper to find renewed purpose. It meant going inside myself to find the answers, and not being afraid to make changes, to take a risk, to fail, to let my family down. I was scared of losing my supportive friends and my self-respect.

Afraid to shed my abuse, as it had become my identity.

I asked myself these questions:

1. What would I do if I knew I couldn't fail?
2. What would I do even if nobody paid me to do it?
3. What makes me come alive and smile again? This time, with a smile on my heart, I knew my purpose would be found.

Discovery of my heartfelt purpose

In my heart, I knew I wanted to speak and write, but the most important part was that I wanted to protect the vulnerable and stop women and children going through the type of pain I experienced. I wanted to consult and mentor, things I would do without asking for payment, with the tremendous validation and satisfaction at the outcomes being more valuable than money.

I would do all the more if I knew I couldn't fail, and if I had a support structure (still lingering in my subconscious mind was the belief that I was a failure), as these were the things that made me fulfilled.

It was love in action for me.

Listening to leaders around the world who had a similar vision and mission, and putting what I had learned into practise, plus adding my own personal experiences, empathy and compassion, I felt raw and real – and excited! – knowing that this was what I loved to do. Although, something was still holding me back, but what?

I know we all want to live in what I call a 'universal assignment,' which is the point at which your talents, skills, abilities and gifts intersect with a void or a need in the world around you. That is, as best I can imagine, the true definition of purpose that we should all aspire to seek. However, like anything else on the journey to success, it isn't a fixed point that you arrive at and stay forever. The world changes too often (mine certainly did). Change is movement, and movement creates different pains, such as growing pains, but the ongoing search for that point can keep us on target.

My desire to know the truth and to learn – my innate curiosity – ignited my mind, forcing it to come alive, away from my history or programming of being a victim.

Authentic confidence leads to authentic motives

I learnt that permanent and real validation comes from within. When your confidence is unshakable and unaffected by the way others react to you, this authentic confidence leads to authentic motives, which creates authentic connections and authentic results.

My confidence increased steadily as I willingly paid the price to develop character and a spirit of excellence. Give instead of take, be kind and care for somebody who cannot do anything for you, simply because you can.

Never let the old lady in

I pursued my inner work, the child within, and faced the external effects by examining my motives, no matter what the situation was, always being truthful to myself to the point that it hurt. By doing otherwise, you risk building your life on an unstable foundation, so rid your system of backstabbing by attempting to control outcomes. I dealt with the bitterness that I had rightfully earned, but did not let it in. I had always vowed I would not become a bitter old lady, and to never let the old lady in.

I discovered that in being obsessed with achieving a particular outcome, I became disconnected from my spirit. Instead, I considered living my life with detached intention, which would be easier, with no more opening up to new pain. Trying deliberately to be aligned with my spirit, this inner peace released my purpose and attracted what was in my best interest, thanks to me being open to different outcomes.

You'll recognise your purpose when time ceases to exist, and there's an alignment of your head, your heart and your hands. Purpose isn't external, it's something you own inside, and I pursued it wholeheartedly.

Intuition is knowing and sensing without the use of rational processes. A hunch, or sixth sense, is when you simply know you were meant to walk a certain path or make a specific decision. You don't know why you know, you just do. **You know with your knower**. This is your internal compass, and I started trusting mine, being much wiser and gradually stronger.

When I let my intuition guide me whilst speaking before a crowd, I fall into a state of uncomplicated joy, knowing that I am making a difference to those people's lives who need to hear. I forget to look at the clock because I am in an effortless flow, doing what I love. Adding value to the truth with love costs me nothing, but will earn me everything. My purpose is to serve those that are willing to try to Live, Love and Laugh again, despite having so much pain and trauma in their past.

My purpose is to serve by being the best version of me

Listening to and following my instincts was the key to becoming purpose-driven. When you live with purpose, you become more intentional about what you do and how you do it.

Whilst many people depend on hard data, schooling and experience to make decisions, I mindfully remain open to what my intuition is telling me, especially if it's different from what my logic indicates.

'Bring us your brains, but check your heart at the door'

I aligned myself with my dream. If you are out of sync with yours, it will not come through. Similarly, if you are operating out of fear, jealously or self-promotion, it will stop you stepping into that purpose.

The times where I simply didn't have enough information to make a good decision, I became quiet, listened to my gut and went with it.

The Three Lighthouses story was always in my mind to guide me.

1. The first lighthouse must make business sense.
2. The second lighthouse must have clarity.
3. The third lighthouse must have peace

Only when all three principles are met can you move forward. I tested this for myself, and now I am making the right decisions.

It is said in a business situation, 'bring us your brains, but check your heart at the door,' but this is not always easy. Whether the world approves or disapproves of you following your intuition, you're the one who has to live with the results of your choices.

You'll know that your instinct is on target by the peace you feel in your soul.

My lifelines

- Keeping moving one step at a time.

- Getting up every morning and giving myself time to grieve the loss of my life and direction.

- Making sure I don't let the victim mentality in.

- Didn't allow myself to be alone for long periods, to avoid depression kicking in.

- Doing the things I love.

- Concentrating on the outcome and not the problem.

- Not talking about it as though it's my default. I have moved on.

- Strengthening my bounce back muscle daily.

- Knowing that going back to past trauma over and over again will hinder me when trying to step into my purpose.

- Focusing on the steps in front of me, not the whole staircase.

- Not worrying what people think, as they don't know how far I've come.

- Not worrying if people don't like me, as most people are struggling to like themselves.

- Marrying my passion to become my true self.

- Operating in fear will stop me from stepping into my purpose.

- Driving my own bus.

- Creating a support system around myself.

- Using my inner peace to create my outer space, ie my impact.

CHAPTER 19

The Curveballs of Life

Curveballs happen

Most day-to-day living, no matter what our home situations are like, comprises good and bad times. Occasionally, life throws us a curveball (a term used in cricket and baseball) to confuse us. We don't see it coming, and have no way of controlling its trajectory.

I have had several situations where I just did not see life's dreaded curveballs coming straight at me, affecting my life on different levels, sometimes with devastating consequences.

We all lead unique lives, so the curveball can be different. It could be a sudden diagnosis of an illness for you or a family member, a sudden death in the family, which none of us can escape from; or perhaps a betrayal leading to divorce, which I most certainly didn't see coming my way.

The sudden state of loneliness that many of us across the world have suffered during the lockdowns and the confusion it created...

Some things that get thrown at your life's path can feel as though they are impossible to get over or out of. The fear and panic of the reality of a situation you are facing has you holding your breath, eyes wide open, asking yourself what now?

Where do you turn when you face these curveballs in your life? What do you say to yourself? The shock and trauma that appear in the blink of an eye can be so destructive that your life may never be the same again.

Do you say "Life sucks," or do you ask yourself how you got into this situation and set about getting out of it?

Similar to potholes, curveballs come out of the blue. Coronavirus, tsunamis, inflation, illness, financial woes and wars are all examples of life's curveballs.

Yes, one solution is not putting yourself out there, playing it safe and staying at home, perhaps being satisfied with an alcoholic drink to provide an easy escape. This may offer temporary relief, but it will not change things or help, that I know. I have seen my fair share of this approach, and it has led to nothing but heartbreak.

The curveballs kept coming, one after the other

Having settled down and got back on my feet again for the most part, I was having my children over for a dinner as normal, and I couldn't but help notice that my son-in-law was not looking well. I asked him what was wrong, and he just said he was tired after a long, busy week. He then very apologetically suggested that he and his family go home straight after dinner, and though I agreed, I was a bit concerned.

Little did I know, this would be the last time I would see him alive.

Whilst still clearing up and doing the dishes, I got a phone call from my daughter.

'Mom, Alan is dead. Come.'

I didn't give an answer.

'Mom!' she repeated, hysteria in her voice now. 'I think Alan has died, come quickly!'

Grabbing my keys, I drove in the pouring rain until I was met by my six-year-old grandson at the security gate. As I tried to cover his little shivering body with my raincoat, I heard him mumbling.

'We have to do something, Granny,' he said desperately. 'We have to do something.'

It was the cry of a child who knew enough to recognise that this was serious, and not the video game kind of dying. This was so real for such a small child, whose only hope was his granny.

We huddled together as we passed through the apartment door, only to find my daughter hysterically trying to resuscitate her husband. Seeing us enter, she began screaming and crying out for me to help him.

Bending over Alan's lifeless body on the stark white tiles of the much-cluttered lounge, I tried CPR several times. His eyes were wide open, and my granddaughter, shivering with a small bath towel wrapped partially around her, having just got out of the bathtub, watched on as her mother frantically called the emergency services and then Alan's parents.

My grandchildren watched their father die, and I couldn't do a thing to protect them from such a traumatic experience.

Kyle and Keira on the night they saw their Father die. I did everything to distract
them, by making an imaginary train with boxes back at my apartment.

The mayhem this imposed on us as a family was catastrophic, and for the next few years, I focussed mainly on my daughter and her children, moving them in to live with me whilst they pieced their lives back together through the grief process.

It was around this time that I got a disturbing message on Facebook from Rick, my first husband's love child, now twenty-one. I responded by saying that I would be phoning him after seven that evening, but this was not to be, as later that afternoon he committed suicide.

Paralyzed with shock, and totally out of myself, I went to my ex-husband's house to ask if he would look after my two border collies for a week. Bearing in mind he had not spoken to me since I fled from him, the first thing he said after I shared with him that Rick had committed suicide was cold in the extreme.

'It serves her right,' he said ('her' being Rick's mother), referring to the fact she had conceived a child with a married man, (my children's father).

I couldn't believe what I had just heard. I was devastated by these harsh, unnecessary words.

'You have a seventeen-year-old son,' I said. 'How could you say that?'

Not expecting an answer, and numbed to any form of feeling, including disgust for the attitude of a man I was once married to, I led the dogs from his garden into my car, which they were quite familiar with.

I still don't know how I could have even expected some form of comfort from this man, who had turned so bitter and self-destructive, hardly recognisable from the person he was when I first met him.

I thought my heart had finally been broken. It would take years for me to heal, as I explain in other chapters.

As a mother and grandmother, I was now totally responsible for looking after my grieving daughter and her two grieving children, so I had no chance to grieve myself. Having just lost millions through the family business (I will expand on this point in, *The Miracles Behind the Smile*; my next book). I now needed to find a place and earn an income for the four of us ASAP.

No house, no transport and no money. It was all up to me.

Two years later, I was alone again in my own place, and all family matters were settling when I was introduced to a Dutch man who needed some administrative work doing. I took on the job, which involved travelling ninety kilometres to his place once a week, and I soon became very involved in his business and the running of his restaurant and farms. We started building a strong bond, and he asked me to accompany him to the cardio specialist's clinic, as I had made the appointment after noticing that he was very out of breath. We never made it to the appointment, however, as the very next day, he was in theatre for an emergency micro valve transplant.

Here I was, running his affairs whilst travelling back and forth for three months, during which time he had two more open heart surgeries. I was getting very involved with his then estranged family, all of whom were against me, as they suspected I was there for his money, even though they only found time to see him once in hospital. I had got myself into a hornets' nest, and it was getting worse by the minute, with legal action and court cases – the lot!

I couldn't in good conscience leave this decent man to face it all alone, and I soon started realising that I had grown very attached to him, which turned into love as he bravely fought for his health. The court cases that followed only brought us closer, and he was hoping that when he got better, we would get married.

That never happened, though, as he died after a third valve replacement.

My heart was broken again, this time so badly that they had to resuscitate me in the bed next to him in the intensive care unit

The following years were horrendous, as the hornets' nest grew bigger with the relentless personal attacks from his family, but I stayed true to myself and did the right thing, plodding along, trying to pick up the pieces of my life. Eventually, the pain subsided and the court cases stopped, as the family kept losing and were advised to come to terms with the situation.

This all happened twelve years ago, and I now understand the anguish and physical pain I felt throughout the recovery of a broken heart, as I fought to get back to wanting to Live, Love and Laugh again. The journey back was embraced slowly, one step at a time; time that I could not rush or force, even though I often wished I could move on. It was a long, long process. More than ten years, in fact.

My fight back muscles were still developing, as I built up the strength to pick myself up again.

My Lifelines

- Be kind to yourself and allow the grieving process
  to take place, no matter how long it takes.

- There is no right or wrong amount of grief.

- Grieving is for any loss of anything, be it a marriage,
  your pet, your health or your business.

- Don't try to understand it right away. Just embrace it.

- Let the tears flow without excuses.

- Finding happiness again is the letting go of every situation
  by recognising and accepting it for what it is.

- To start again was not an option, so I just got on with it.

- A little progress every day builds momentum.

- Giving myself the time to feel, the space to cry and the hope
  it would heal took a lot of courage and willpower.

> *No Matter how bad your heart is broken, the world
> doesn't stop for your grief . Faraaz Kazi*

CHAPTER 19

Stepping Out of the Boat and Learning to Swim Again

Why am I making the same mistakes?

Here I go into overdrive, internally and physically, to find my deepest unknown

A sking myself, what is wrong with me, and in real terms, is there anything right with me?

I was being very hard on myself, as being self-critical is a form of accepting the abuse and all the lies that comes with it. I would think small, even going so far as loathing myself. The tears started to dry up – 'It's all my fault' – not obvious to others, but definitely showing its ugly head in my body language and self-confidence, and certainly in my decision making, as I'd stop and then start up again in my life.

Have I got low self-esteem? I wondered. *Is this why I cannot attract someone good as life partner?*

I didn't like myself. My lack of self-love had blinded me to the fact that the past abuse I had suffered was what I had attracted in, perhaps subconsciously failing to recognise my value by going after men who don't treat me well and were unable to make me happy.

I subconsciously didn't want to be involved with anyone. This was a deep inner 'vow' that I had made to myself, declaring that I would never be able to be good enough or happy, probably because I was abused as a child, and not aware of it until the age of fifty-five.

Am I damaged goods? I asked myself. I'll come right out and say it, I believe I am damaged. That doesn't make me a bad person, but the result is that I was stuck in a pattern, as there is a subconscious comfort in the familiarity, even when it involves abuse, and this prevented me from realising that I needed to break this awful pattern in order to attract a different kind of man.

Harsh though it may sound, every divorced person (and, really, anybody who is older and has lived a life) is going to be damaged in some way, but I didn't want to stay single for the rest of my life, lonely and sad, which explains why I was settling.

Recognising a pattern, but too ashamed to face it

This was the hardest part for me to face, as I had to come to terms with all the above, step by step and layer by layer, something like peeling an onion. Sometimes, with tears of healing and pain at the same time, finding the relief and solace, and being able to move on. This I did with the help of counselling, and the will to stop the craziness of my life in the hope of getting it right eventually.

The mistakes I made will not define me. It's what I do with them that makes all the difference

There has to come a point in any situation where you have had enough; when you actually say to yourself, 'That's it, enough is enough,' and you mean it.

I reached that point, becoming stronger than that which had happened to me. I could not keep carrying the load, and had to stand up and face the music, no matter what the pain of my now would be. I needed to take the plunge by stepping out of the boat and learning to walk on water, straight into my unfamiliar and the unknown, putting a stop to the madness that was consuming me.

I had to take stock

I reached the point where I could see that I was always accepting, and subconsciously planning for, defeat. I had to change my battle plan and choose when to fight to win the war and become a conqueror, not conquered, by my day-to-day situation; to choose to no longer be a victim of circumstance imposed upon me, but to rise up and be a victor in my life.

I made the biggest decision of my life

I phoned my son in the UK and said, 'I am coming to the UK as soon as I can.'

'Come again, Mom?' he gulped, as if he didn't hear me the first time.

'I am coming to London as soon as possible,' I said, softening my voice, 'to start my new life.'

There was a silence before he spoke again.

'Mom... I welcome you here... if you are serious about this.'

'It will be as soon as I have packed up and sold what I can. Then, I will be there.'

I was talking myself into it, not allowing doubt to creep in, as I started to plan.

Leaving all I knew behind me at age sixty-five and setting off to a foreign country to start all over again, alone, was a daunting prospect, but change never frightened me, even when it was as drastic and final as this.

The following day, I resigned from my job and sold all I could get rid of at a garage sale two weeks later. This was me going sailing, but in a motor boat at full throttle, with no idea of how the next step would pan out or how I would ever earn my keep or cope. The implications were really final, as I had no recourse to go back to South Africa except for holidays. My grandchildren were confused, and one of my daughters was really trying to manipulate me into believing that this was a bad decision. Meanwhile, the sadness and emotion of letting go, not to mention my grandchildren's questions about whether I'd be back for school concerts or birthdays, was not making my decision any easier.

I pulled it off, though.

Within a month, I was at the airport, saying goodbye to my children, grandchildren and my two dogs (which was very hard, as they were such a source of comfort in my darkest times). None of them understood why I was doing this, and neither did I, but I was laser-focussed on my new life in London.

Saying goodbye to four of my grandchildren before starting a new life in the UK

London, here I come! My whole life was crammed into one 32kg suitcase, as I unapologetically went about starting fresh. I left Africa, which I love with a passion, alone to embrace London and all its challenges and unknowns, understanding that if I looked back and compared – or even dwelt on my grandchildren and all the precious moments I would be missing out on, never mind my dogs and the weather being so different – I would risk faltering in my conviction.

Embracing the fast pace of living in the UK, travelling underground and still seeing trees, and questioning my son as to how this was possible; getting on the Circle Line and going around in circles, not sure where to get off, to the amusement of my friends; and learning to Google everything and to travel everywhere by foot, bus or train... It was quite an adjustment, having always had my own car in the past. I also had to get rid of all the clothes and shoes I arrived with, as they were totally unsuitable for the new life I was starting.

Change was inevitable, as charity shops and living out of a single room in a house share with four very young people became my new life, but I dared not complain. I was here for a purpose, so fully embraced every new thing, adjusting so well that I soon became a public speaker and started my own online business.

Learning to keep up with various online courses on self-improvement, I was growing and transforming on my way to becoming an international bestselling author, and now I have published this book, *Tears Behind the Smile.*

Not yet arrived, but striving to learn and be more like who I truly am, learning to swim again. I wake up with determination and go to bed with satisfaction, one day at a time, celebrating my small achievements.

I was willing to acknowledge the path I had to walk, and believed I could create a new life by stepping intentionally into that reality, freely giving up what was no longer serving me.

> *If you don't get out of the boat, you can't walk on water or learn to swim, and you will never find the treasures of life yet for you to discover.*

My Lifelines

- Embracing the unknown is a mindset of expecting growth and pain to find a good end result.

- The first step to getting anywhere is deciding that you're not willing to stay where you are.

- Make a decision, keep moving and don't look back.

- Don't take yourself too seriously, and enjoy the journey.

- Being keen to change and learning new things makes change so much easier.

- Embrace the new and let go of the old.

- Have a vision and a purpose to the outcome, even if it's not that clear.

- Choose to improve the mistakes you make, and stop being so hard on yourself.

- Embrace the unfamiliar and walk towards it.

- Surround yourself with new like-minded people.

- By committing to yourself first, you will get your best results.

- Accept that your path is bigger than yourself.

- Stay true to yourself, and remember your roots.

- Always encourage yourself by finding your
  truth and not living the lie.

- To live again, to laugh again, to try again and to start
  again. To fight back, whatever life may throw you.

- Whats and the hows are only steps towards beginning again.

- Learning the how to make my wow.

- Never swim against the current, as the current will
  take you in the flow of finding your answer.

- Knowing change is never easy, but it is going to be worth it.

- Remembering the best view comes after the hardest climb.

- Raise yourself higher than your greatest fear and see what happens.

- Live in truth, expressing the highest, truest version of yourself.

- We have the resources within. Your heart will tell you the way to go.

- Surround yourself with people that fill your cup.

- Success is not your value and does not define you.
  It is how you share and serve that does.

- Be intentional towards your outcome with
  every step and direction you take.

Wisdom Wise

'What happens to an open wound, apart from getting infected? It becomes a nice target for another time. If there is an unhealed hurt, I will go out of my way, unconsciously, and get hurt in the same spot again. It is bound to happen. That's what happens to the trauma that people like me have. It never heals, and can keep attracting trauma in a different form.'

JOKÉ HOETMER

CHAPTER 20

From Pain to Pearls

**The transformation of pain and
difficulty can, with time, result in
a greater hope and expectation,
by learning to trust again**

Like everybody else, my life has been made up of circumstances
and experiences that have determined my future. I had to learn
from those times when figuring out the next move and how to
approach my future. It all depended on me; with only the thoughts and
scars that I had to bear and the lessons I learned to guide me.

I decided to choose joy, and didn't wait around for circumstances to
become better, easier or in real terms simpler. We all know that life
can be complicated and has its ups and downs, as nobody is immune to
its happenings, like a game of snakes and ladders. It's how we choose
to embrace the losses and challenges it presents that will define our
todays and our tomorrows.

You cannot plan for defeat and expect victory. Something had to change

I learned to embrace the now. No more looking over my shoulder, expecting the worst, but embracing hope for a brighter outcome to my decision making. Throughout my rollercoaster journey, I had to believe that life gives second chances, otherwise I would have never got out of bed, landing myself in depression. I had to learn that there are some people who always seem angry and are continuously looking for conflict. I knew I couldn't change that – it isn't in my jurisdiction – and that they have their own journeys to walk. Their salvation is not mine to provide, nor mine theirs. We each stand accountable for our own life decisions and their consequences. This was one of the most profound lessons I had to learn. **You are what you believe.**

I chose to walk away, as **the battle they were fighting isn't with me, but within themselves. I kept on reminding myself who I was and chose to forget who they said I was, that was the start of my freedom.**

> *'It's your road and yours alone. Others may walk it with you, but no one can walk it for you.'* – **Rumi**

Post-it Notes of Second Chances

Find the courage and strength, and dare to rise again (DARE TO CARE), rising to the next challenge.

I embraced my second chances by reading these quotes, and then writing them on post-it notes and sticking them all over the house on mirrors, the fridge and my computer, acting as a constant reminder.

My Second Chances and Reminders

- **Design your will to embrace yourself, integrating the past into your present.**

- **Pursue your instinct to be yourself, and shine your light to make the difference.**

- **Love yourself for yourself, so you can love others unconditionally.**

- **Do not take yourself seriously. You should, however, take life seriously.**

- **Live out the truest, highest version of yourself.**

- Do not be afraid to laugh at yourself. It puts a
  smile on your face, and others will follow.

- Smile, even if there is nothing to smile about.

- Embrace your flaws. They are the unique scars of your beauty.

- Release what no longer serves you and
  create the space that inspires you.

- Rule your mind, don't let it rule you.

- Listen to your inner voice and act on it, before you
  get a chance to doubt that you heard it.

- You are unique. Be the best version of
  yourself, as that will always be great.

- You are perfect just the way you are, and see how your
  smile creeps up at the corners of your mouth.

- Seize the moment to do the right thing, even
  when it does not make sense.

- Stay true to your heritage, and always
  remember where you came from.

- Live your life in and through truth, and you will survive anything.

- Remember, there is a power greater than yourself, trust that.

- Lead by example when nobody is watching.

- Stop comparing yourself with other people. It will never work.

- Being yourself is a gift to others.

- The number one job is to grow yourself into the best possible version.

- Never be afraid to laugh at yourself by putting a smile on your face.

- Shine your light in the darkness that is trying to overwhelm and dim your true self.

- You can connect to that source and discover your true identity, purpose and power.

- Make time and space for your purpose, and step into making a difference to one person at a time, creating a tidal wave of impact and power.

- Focus on the steps in front of you, not the whole staircase.

- Stay in your core value at all times. Do not compromise.

- To master your talent, only you can be you.

- Give without expecting anything in return, and sow a seed just to see it grow.

- Know your choice of direction by aligning yourself with life's manual, the Bible.

- Marry your passion, be true to yourself, as therein lays the power of making an impact.

- Try looking at yourself and into your future to create the motion of purpose by enabling you to become the best version of yourself and to achieve your greatest aspirations.

- Believe in the highest level of yourself, as there is a power greater and bigger than yourself.

- Connect yourself to the force higher than yourself, and keep connected to that higher power.

- Believing in your divine, you step into your perfect self.

- Once your cup is full, you can pour out fully to others.

- Be a warrior of the light and live in the light of Faith, Hope and Love.

- Never envy somebody else's success, as they may have their own tears behind their own smiles.

- Your own fate and adventures are more than enough to walk in, so always try to be true to yourself on your journey, to be the best version of you.

"You cannot go back and change the beginning, but you can start where you are, and change the ending." – C.S. Lewis

CHAPTER 21

The Love Story

I finally found the man I could love and trust, who is able to love me for who I am, knowing my past in full, and able to live, love and laugh again in my now

L ife happens. Mine has certainly had its fair share of unfortunate things occurring, some because I just happened to be in the wrong place at the wrong time, which was in reality some of my own making, but the pendulum can swing the other way just as quickly.

The journey from there was the childlike freshness with the butterflies in your stomach kind. At our age, not possible, surely?

I never stopped hoping to find my true match, a man that can handle me as I am, being a redhead who is now a greying blonde. The fire, fight and will for the real thing always burning in my soul, something like a chocolate toffee éclair, all tough on the outside, but with a soft centre. You see, I had learned to hide the real woman inside; not from my friends, of course, but from the men out there.

Slowly, as my soul was being healed and I was being restored, I was coming out of that self-protection facade, having a big plastic bubble around me and being inside it for all to see, but not allowing anybody to get too close.

As I got to the age of seventy, I was starting to give up my hope of finding my forever partner. It was as if I had a clear view of what I was and what I needed, as well as what I didn't want. I knew I was healed of the trauma, and had accepted my misjudgement and choices; the lies

I had believed, and the truths that were hidden behind the romance or the physical. Accepting and then forgiving them and myself was continuously a process, until today. After mostly wasting the best years of my life, I had to let go of those thoughts, as well as other concerns about being too old and damaged goods.

These were the negative destructive thoughts I had to continually fight, all the while still hoping that my fulfilment with a life partner would happen. I THOUGHT I WOULD NEVER BE READY FOR MY OWN MR RIGHT, BUT CONTINUED HOPING ANYWAY, so I kept one eye open in case, maybe possibly perhaps???

Then, one day, I saw this very English man. Me being Dutch and having lived in Africa most of my life, I was certainly not the typical lady for this man, who had the most endearing smile.

So, I waved.

Yes, it started with a wave, a meeting and oh, so formal. Then, the smile and, days later, with the kiss.

Wow, oh Wow! Giggle!

The journey from there was the childlike freshness with the butterflies in your stomach kind. At our age (Paul 70 and me 72), not possible, surely?

Over the next few months, we got to know each other quite rapidly, as he was reading the draft chapters of this book, *Tears Behind the Smile*. He loved me even more because of what I had gone through, which made me the person he sees and experiences now.

The reason we got to know each other so naturally was that he also had a past he was not proud of, having known similar business and relationship failures. Like me, he understood the power of the lessons learned, and the continuous hope that we'll eventually get it right.

We both now know what we want, and how to treasure the good and swim through the tough times, only to come out stronger and wiser. We are strong united, and pulling together towards our future with experience of pain and brokenness in one hand, and hope and laughter in the other.

I now have the laughter in my heart that makes me smile, as we set out on our exciting journey together.

Just a month before Tears Behind The Smile was published, we were married. Paul is my biggest supporter to help both women and men with their brokenness and healing, Just what I needed at last. SMILE!

> *Don't judge me by my journey, judge me by my destination, and remember that for yourselves. We All Have a Past, with a sincere Hope for a Future.*

My Lifelines

- Love yourself for yourself, so you can love others unconditionally.

- Choose to love, remembering nobody is perfect.

- Try looking at yourself in the mirror and seeing the future you.

- Stop comparing yourself to there. It will never work; it's a lie that can destroy you.

- Being yourself is a gift to your life partner and others.

- Open your heart space to love more.

- Love life, and life will love you back.

- Raise yourself higher than your greatest fear and see what happens.

- This is your time to shine. If the GOD of the universe is for you, who can be against you?

- Fulfil the highest expression of yourself.

- Always strive to give 100%. Remember its never too late to start over!

> *Mr or Mrs Perfect, are they out there?*
> *Prepare yourself as though they are*

Note for a new relationship:
Do not tell a man what you desire. The right one
will know exactly what to do and when to do it.

CHAPTER 22

A Reason for Every Season

Hope always prevails, this is only a season, and there is a reason for the season and a lesson to learn. What is the lesson right now, for any woman or man reading this book today?

Find the reason, and learn the lessons in that season

How many of the following lifelines can you identify with and embrace, to help you on your journey of finding your self-worth and confidence to be the real you again?

1. I am going to make the choice to change my circumstances and find the way out.
2. Never be rushed into deciding when you are in the middle of a storm.
3. You have the answer deep within you, just find it.
4. Find the Lie, the Truth and the Choice.
5. Find the smile to find your heart again.

6. Stop, breathe, don't assume, don't react... the answer will come.
7. You got this!
8. Life is like lollipop; you never know what's inside.
9. I have the choice, so I can make it now.
10. Whatever is in your hand, your heart and your desire to give your all, will carry the power to be your fulfilment and purpose.
11. See the outcome, and work towards it.
12. This is not what defines me, so I will not let it in.
13. I choose to forgive myself first before I can move on.
14. I have the guts and the will to face this.
15. I've got this covered.
16. Nobody defines me but myself.
17. Shame and Blame does not suit me.
18. I am worth it.
19. I am not going to be Defined or Defeated by the wrong choices I have made.
20. I have the Power Within me to Change.
21. I have the will and the resilience to bounce back.
22. I am not broken, I have just experienced life.
23. **I am not broken-hearted, I am just expressing the love I have lost.**
24. Loss is only temporary, as I know a new thing is going to be awesome.
25. Feel into it. If it feels right and makes sense, step towards it.
26. What have I to lose by trying. If I don't try, I will never know.
27. Life happens and curveballs are thrown your way, but you are never alone or the only one that has had this happen to.
28. Life sucks, but don't be a sucker.
29. Learn to Decide, Discern and Distract yourself through the chaos.
30. Remember to keep movement in your life, as movement means that you are growing.
31. Feel the fear and do it anyway.
32. **Love is never perfect, otherwise it's not love.**
33. People come and go, just let them go.
34. There is no Mr Right, only Mr Right Now.
35. If I want to be loved for being me, the question is: do I love myself?

36. Don't look for Mr or Miss Right, look at how you can prepare yourself for the right person.
37. Relationships start with loving yourself.
38. Just show up. You never know what's around the corner.
39. Stop worrying about what others think of you, as they are too busy thinking about themselves.
40. If you allow shame and blame in, you are giving them residence in your house.
41. Allowing the predator to shame you only gives him or her the power to define you.
42. **The past does not define you, it has only shaped you towards your future and purpose.**
43. It's not what you say, but your actions that matter.
44. If you find you are the common denominator then look at the problem within yourself.
45. I am who I am by loving and respecting yourself in all of You.
46. Love unconditionally, forgive continuously and be willing to learn from the lessons thrown before you and you will succeed.
47. Be aware that the ripple effect you have will never be known to you, so walk through life wisely.
48. You will never be ready or good enough, so why not act now?
49. Life's chances are just a decision away.
50. Help! I need somebody to help me. Never be afraid to ask, as you will be surprised at how much help is out there.
51. Instead of 'if only,' say 'I Can and I Will.'
52. You decide to be free. To continue looking back will stop you moving towards your future.
53. Let go and move forward.
54. Step up and step out.
55. To make a difference to those around you, you need to show up.

I now always have the power to choose and the power of letting go, and the ability to step into the power of My NOW

The reality of Domestic Abuse Worldwide

World Health Organisation Figures

- Violence against women – particularly intimate partner violence and sexual violence – is a major public health problem and a violation of women's human rights.
- Estimates published by WHO indicate that globally about 1 in 3 (30%) women worldwide have been subjected to either physical and/or sexual intimate partner violence or non-partner sexual violence in their lifetime.
- Most of this violence is intimate partner violence. Worldwide, almost one third (27%) of women aged 15-49 years who have been in a relationship report that they have been subjected to some form of physical and/or sexual violence by their intimate partner.
- Violence can negatively affect women's physical, mental, sexual, and reproductive health, and may increase the risk of acquiring HIV in some settings.
- Violence against women is preventable. The health sector has an important role to play to provide comprehensive health care to women subjected to violence, and as an entry point for referring women to other support services they may need.
- Most violence against women is perpetrated by current or former husbands or intimate partners. More than 640 million women aged 15 and older have been subjected to intimate partner violence (26 per cent of women aged 15 and older).
- Of those who have been in a relationship, almost one in four adolescent girls aged 15–19 (24 per cent) have experienced physical and/or sexual violence from an intimate partner or husband. Sixteen per cent of young women aged 15 to 24 experienced this violence in the past 12 months.
- In 2018, an estimated one in seven women had experienced physical and/or sexual violence from an intimate partner or husband in the past 12 months (13 per cent of women aged 15–49). These numbers do not reflect the impact of the COVID-19 pandemic, which has increased risk factors for violence against women.

- The Office of National Statistics reported in the United Kingdom alone, Police recording a total of 1,459,663 domestic abuse-related incidents and crimes in England and Wales in the year ending March 2021. Of these, 845,734 were recorded as domestic abuse-related crimes, an increase of 6% from the previous year, representing 18% of all offences recorded by the police in the year ending March 2021.
- Estimates from the ONS' most recent Crime Survey for England and Wales year ending March 2020 show 5.5% of adults aged 16 to 74 years (2.3 million) experienced domestic abuse in the prior 12 months.
- In one major City on the south coast of England, Police report that if the local football (Soccer) team lose, Domestic violence increases by a staggering 60%.

> *The more that we can identify what is particularly true for us individually, the more we may discover that other women are making similar journeys, and that there is help if we reach out.*

JOKÉ HOETMER

I made this my declaration of MY independence

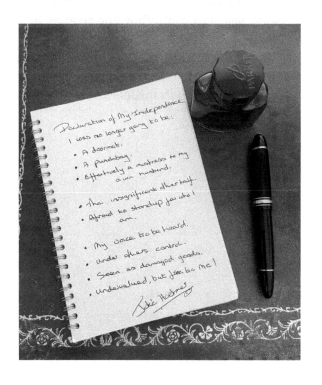

I was no longer going to be...

- A doormat
- A Punchbag
- Effectively a mistress to my own husband
- The insignificant other half
- Afraid to stand up for who I am
- A voice never heard
- Under others' control
- Damaged goods
- Undervalued, as I am free to be ME

So, perhaps the best way to predict your own future is to start creating it for yourself. If not today, when? Your future is literally in your hands when you start controlling and creating it

Never plan your future based on your past. Grieve for your past without bringing its mistakes into your future

My Question and challenge for You:

Has suffering in your life bred bitterness, resentment leading to some form of addiction? Or has your suffering produced endurance, which produces and develops your character, your individuality, and then can produce a hope that you will never be disappointed in.

Consider how you might use your own journey of suffering and endurance to encourage others on their journeys. Please join me and make a difference, wherever, and whenever you can.

JOKÉ HOETMER

Note

Publishing in early 2023 is Joké's second book,
The Miracles Behind the Smile, in which she tells the
story of the miracles that kept her going, and how she
came through the tests that created her testimony.

JOKÉ HOETMER

Lightning Source UK Ltd.
Milton Keynes UK
UKHW021822151122
412254UK00011B/747